D0121762

BETWEEN TWO WORLDS: A Congressman's Choice

John B. Anderson

THIRD-RANKING REPUBLICAN IN THE U.S. HOUSE OF REPRESENTATIVES

BETWEEN TWO WORLDS: A Congressman's Choice

Zondervan Publishing House
Grand Rapids, Michigan

To my wife

KEKE

who throughout the years of
my public career has devoted
herself lovingly to the tasks as
wife and mother which have truly
blessed my private life.

CONTENTS

FOREWORD

INTRODUCTION

FOREWORD

This is a book about institutions and issues. Since Lord Bryce and Alexis de Toqueville, innumerable writers, both American and foreign, have contributed to the floodtide of literature on the subject of American institutions. The issues — social, economic and political — that presently confront American society have also scarcely been neglected by contemporary writers.

In addition to a discussion of institutions and issues, this book is concerned with a third "I": individual perspective. It has taken at least a decade to write, for it is very largely based on the experiences and observations which I have gained over that period of time while serving in the Congress of the United States. Other men have served for longer than that and written of their experiences, so perhaps I have not yet suggested any good and sufficient reason why this book has appeared.

However, in furnishing this individual perspective on contemporary American institutions and issues, I was motivated by a desire to discuss them from the vantage point of my own personal religious faith and Christian commitment.

As the title of this book implies, I believe that we are embarked upon a journey between two worlds. In essence it is the journey of which John Bunyan wrote in his great classic, *Pilgrim's Progress*. There is the world into which we were born, and the world of which Emily Dickinson spoke in one of her verses,

> I never spoke with God,
> Nor visited in Heaven;
> Yet certain am I of the spot
> As if the chart were given . . .

There are difficult choices which we must make in many different areas as we pursue our earthly pilgrimage. My experience is in the political arena where I daily participate in the decision-making process of our national government. If in some small measure this book serves to define the critical issues of our time and helps illumine the choices which we as Christians must make, I will feel richly rewarded for the effort and the investment of time that it represents. For time and again during His short thirty-three years on this earth, our Lord demonstrated His positive stand on the issues of His day. He was constantly aware of both the physical and the spiritual needs of all those to whom He ministered. I believe that He likewise expects those who are called by His name to show the same concern and to live and act decisively on the problems of our time.

I am indebted to many people for their assistance in the preparation of this manuscript. It had its origins in a number of tape-recorded sessions with James Reapsome, when we discussed at length some of the ideas which eventually found their way into these pages. I am extremely grateful to him for this help as well as the advice and suggestions he offered in the preparation of the first draft. Bob DeVries consistently offered his encouragement and inspired us with his enthusiasm at those crucial moments when our own had begun to falter. My thanks go also to Dorothy Holley, who transformed page after page of illegible longhand into a neatly-typed manuscript.

Most of all I wish to acknowledge an enormous debt to my administrative assistant, Howard Moffett, whose help was truly indispensable. He brought to his task the qualities of an incisive mind and impressive scholarship together with deeply shared concerns about the necessity of a positive Christian perspective on contemporary issues and institutions. Without his determination to help me see the job through, I am convinced that this book, like the world before creation, would in the words of Genesis still be "without form and void."

I have learned that the leap from the political stump to the author's chair is fraught with great peril. Therefore, I am also indebted to the publishers, Zondervan, for their faith in an untried author and their patience in so many different matters where their forbearance and cooperation was required.

Washington, D.C.
July 20, 1970

INTRODUCTION

At the time of this writing anyone looking at the state of our world recognizes the need for reconciliation at every level, and the urgent need for justice and peace throughout our world. There are deep rifts among the different segments of society in many nations, and violent conflicts engulfing whole areas of the globe. The United States is involved in the longest war of her history. She has lost about 50,000 young people, and the hostilities have spread through all of Indochina. There are at least twenty-two active insurrections throughout the world. These involve such countries as Burma, Cambodia, Columbia, The Congo, Angola, India, Indonesia, Iraq, Malaysia, Portuguese Guinea and Ireland. All of these emit sparks that could ignite a great conflagration.

Due to the increased intensity of communication through television, radio, and the newspapers, it has become apparent to men in all parts of the world that we have not achieved the ability to live together as brothers. The question therefore arises, "How long can we tolerate conflict which erupts into distrust, lack of understanding, and hate as a norm for every-day living?" In other generations it was possible to sweep our collective sins under the rug, but today students and young people throughout the world are deeply aware and involved in these situations. The inability of their fathers, their mothers and the leaders of nations to cope with this problem of alienation has created a disillusionment which is becoming increasingly impossible to overcome through any human means, including the force of arms.

The need of the hour, as I see it, is for men who can fill the vacuum of leadership throughout the world and confront these challenges.

For this reason I am most grateful for *Between Two Worlds: A Congressman's Choice*, because I believe that in John Anderson we have such a man. In biblical history we read in Ezekiel how God sought a man who would "stand in the gap" and represent Him and His concerns before a nation. It seems as though God has always sought out certain men who would stand for Him to achieve His purposes. We know that the destiny of men and nations for good or ill resides in the hands of relatively few men. While men are always looking for better methods, God is always looking for better men. It is my hope that those who read this book will not only see John Anderson but will also sense the underlying principles, values and ways of thinking which undergird his life and have given to it such quality and strength of character.

Despite these great problems which plague our age, I, like John Anderson, am not a nihilist. I do not believe that the world is so gloomy that all we can do is to prepare for our inevitable doom. Rather, I suggest that there are concrete sources of hope for the future.

First, there is an increased capacity to communicate that can broaden our understanding and better our human relations. Properly used and in the hands of men of good will, this revolution of communications can bridge gaps between men of all nations, diminishing violence and injecting instead enthusiasm, purpose and hope. The new communications techniques can become a practical instrument for developing true brotherhood in our global village.

Secondly, there is hope, because the youth of the world are becoming united. They do not accept the barriers and the fences which have driven mankind apart. They are uniting and discovering by experience and observation that unless all men find a way to work together, there is no hope for them. Even though they may not be approaching the problem through religious convictions, they are coming to know that the world will not function correctly unless man learns to love his fellowman in the same way that God so loved the world that He would not have any man perish. If my observations are correct about the climate among young people of the day, the adult generation has an unusual opportunity to provide the right kind of leadership in this hour.

The third great hope is the challenge to mobilize not only the vast natural resources of the world but the vast human resources. People are created for companionship. There is a great desire within the hearts of all men to unite together and work together for something true and right and good. In order to accomplish this mobilization we must learn to live together. We must learn to understand each other's cultural backgrounds. We must learn to see things from another's point of view. We must learn to let nothing be done through strife or selfishness. We must learn to esteem others greater than ourselves.

The reason why I mention these potential sources of hope is that I want to emphasize that for men who will dare to go against the tide, there are great resources available with which to form solutions to the problems that confront us.

John Anderson has frequently chosen to go against the tide of popular opinion and conventional wisdom because of deeper conviction.

You will find throughout this book a candid portrayal of the struggle of one man seeking to reconcile his understanding of what God wants in the world with what actually is. His solutions may not always be yours, but I believe you should seek to understand the basic motivations and principles that are guiding him.

You will also find a definitive statement of his views on the structures and institutions of our country and well-thought-out explanations of why he feels certain programs can be a help in meeting our problems.

In the following chapters we find a man who has taken time to set forth his purposes and objectives and has done sufficient homework so that he can articulate his means of achieving them. Even though we may choose other purposes and perhaps other parties and institutions as our model, this book challenges us to re-think our own direction.

Finally, I would like to say that perhaps the greatest single contribution that John Anderson has made, not only to the lives of those men and women who have known him, but perhaps to other nations and to the world, is that he demonstrates a balance of faith and action which should characterize the lives of all who share our faith. Perhaps this was best described by Henry Carter when speaking of John Wesley: "To Wesley a scheme to reconstruct society which ignored the redemption of the individual was unthinkable, but a doctrine to save sinning men, with no aim to transform them into crusaders against social sin was equally unthinkable."

Some preach the gospel of social concern, others preach the Gospel of personal salvation. John Anderson's words and life demonstrate clearly to those of us who will listen that Jesus Christ has the power and desire to redeem the whole man, that indeed the love of God must involve every aspect of our being. John Anderson is seeking to convey that if we have not had an encounter that involves our total selves, then we have not had the true encounter that God means us to have.

It is my conviction that there is no situation in the world in which Jesus Christ is not relevant. I am grateful to be associated in a common brotherhood with a Congressman who is commited to Jesus Christ and dedicated to service in a world that yearns for reconciliation.

The Honorable Mark O. Hatfield
United States Senator

ORIGINS

As its title suggests, this is a book about choices. In these first few chapters, I would like to set the stage for the discussion of institutions and issues which follows by giving the reader some idea of the way in which one Congressman approaches these choices in his daily work.

In the first chapter I have tried to provide an introduction to the world of the Congress by focusing on what has been, for me, the most dramatic choice of my own Congressional career. The second and third chapters are given to a brief discussion of origins — my own background in northwestern Illinois and the decisions that finally led me to a seat in the House of Representatives. Chapter four is intended to give some idea of what it is like to be a Congressman, as a warning to any reader who might be thinking of running for office himself. The final chapter of this section is a discussion of how a Congressman who is also a committed Christian tries to reconcile, in his daily choices, the multifarious demands of constituents, colleagues, outside pressure groups, and his own conscience.

1
ONE
VOTE
CAN
MAKE A
DIFFERENCE

Washington was in turmoil. Acrid fumes of smoke lay heavy in the air, and orange fires licked at the sky across portions of the city's northwest sector. A few blocks from the United States Capitol, angry crowds swept through the downtown ghetto. Entire blocks were virtually devastated and, inevitably, there was a tragic toll of human life as arson and looting became the consequence of the prevailing mob spirit.

Early the evening before — on Thursday, 4 April 1968 — Martin Luther King had been assassinated in Memphis, Tennessee. The nation's capital, its population more than sixty percent black, had been thrown into a convulsion of rioting, arson, and looting, by this news. A curfew had been imposed, and National Guard and Army troops had been called out to restore order. I will never forget the sensation of looking down from the white-columned portico of the House of Representatives and seeing a young army private in combat fatigues manning a fifty-caliber machine gun — to defend, if necessary, the makers of his nation's laws.

The Negro revolution and the civil rights movement had been building for more than a decade, ever since the young Dr. King had led the 1956 bus boycott in Montgomery, Alabama. But only in the 1960's did the full impact of this great and divisive issue burst upon the national scene in all its fury. The student sit-ins began in North Carolina in 1960, the year I was first elected to Congress. In 1963 came the March on Washington and the Birmingham church bombings. The next summer there were civil rights murders in the South and ugly race riots in the North. Congress passed the historic Civil Rights Act of 1964 and the Voting Rights Act of 1965. Still the violence and hatred spread; in succeeding summers, Los Angeles, Chicago, Cleveland, Newark, and Detroit were the scenes of fiery disorders.

Now Washington was the focal point of long pent-up passions. Though I did not realize it at the time, events were rushing toward what was to be for me the single most dramatic incident of my years in Congress, and a crisis of Christian conscience.

A few weeks earlier, the Civil Rights Act of 1968 had come before the House of Representatives. It had originated in the House in 1967 as a relatively mild civil rights bill, providing for penalties against persons convicted of interfering with the civil rights of others. Its authors were simply hoping to put something on the federal statute books that could be used in cases like the 1964 civil rights murder in Philadelphia, Mississippi.

But after it passed the House, the bill went to the Senate for consideration early in 1968. There it was redrafted, enlarged, and changed almost completely to include a title on open housing — providing for federal penalties against anyone who refused to rent or sell property to another person because of race, color, or creed. There were exceptions for single family residences and so on, but, basically, it was a Federal Open Housing statute, with all that this implied. It was one of the most inflammatory issues that had come before the Congress during my tenure. The outbreaks of violence in various parts of the country had greatly heightened the controversy over the open housing issue, which had, of course, been raised in previous Congresses, notably the 88th and 89th.

Normally when there is a difference between House and Senate versions of the same bill, both chambers send representatives to a House-Senate Conference to iron out the differences and produce a bill acceptable to both bodies. But because of the urgency of this issue, many House members now wanted to adopt an abbreviated form of legislative procedure, accepting the strong Senate version of the bill and by-passing the House-Senate Conference.

Virtually all important legislation that comes before the House must first be granted a "rule" by the Rules Committee, a resolution specifying the time limits and other conditions for debate on the floor. The question that came before the Committee on 19 March 1968 — two weeks before Dr. King's death — was whether to adopt and send to the floor of the House a resolution accepting the Senate bill, including the controversial open housing provisions, or to adopt a resolution sending the Senate bill to a House-Senate Conference, where its strongest provisions might be eliminated or watered down.

The crucial Rules Committee vote on the resolution was set for Tuesday, April 9. It would occur only after some days of hearings before the Committee. I had served on the Rules Committee since 1963, but never had I been so torn in trying to decide how to cast my vote. The Committee was controlled by the Democrats, ten to five, but this was to be an issue on which party lines would be broken. It gradually became clear to me that my vote might be the deciding one.

There were some very powerful reasons for voting to send the bill to Conference. I come from an area in northwestern Illinois where the political climate was not particularly hospitable to legislation of this kind. The 16th District was only about seven percent black. I had received literally scores of letters from constituents, urging me to vote against an open housing bill because it would violate the fundamental right of contract, the right of individuals to dispose of their property as they saw fit. And if you destroyed property rights and contract rights, you were laying siege to the very foundations of our Republic — so the argument went.

On a similar open housing question in 1966, I had voted with the majority on the Rules Committee against the provision. The other four Republican Committee members were now prepared to vote against accepting the Senate bill, and many observers expected that I would vote as I had two years before. In addition, I did feel that some provisions of the Senate bill had been hurriedly drafted, and for that reason, when it first came before the Rules Committee on March 19, I had voted with the other members of my party to delay its consideration by the House. Finally, I was personally approached by the Minority Leader and other Senior House Republicans who asked me to vote to send the bill to Conference.

But I was also approached by others, distinctly in the minority, who urged me to vote favorably on the proposition of open housing. Their argument was that, given the racial division in our country, given the problems and conditions I have described, the only hope for some reconciliation between the races lay in opening to black people the opportunity to improve their lot in life. A necessary first step would be to give them equal access to better housing on a nondiscriminatory basis.

The open housing advocates opposed sending the Senate bill to Conference for two reasons. First, in the legislative infighting and tough bargaining over controversial provisions, many of the strongest guarantees in the bill might be softened or even knocked out completely. Second, if the bill were to be sent to Conference, it would then have to be ratified again by both Houses, opening up the possibility of another Senate filibuster which could kill the bill.

3

For days I read and listened to views on both sides, argued with myself, and went through an agony of questioning, resolve, doubt, and prayer. The telephone rang constantly. Telegrams and letters kept pouring in. I was short of sleep and short of temper. But toward the end of the week preceding the vote in the Rules Committee, the major strains in the arguments seemed to sort themselves out in my mind, and I found myself leaning toward a vote to accept the Senate bill with its strong open housing provisions. Four factors seemed especially important.

First, witnesses before the Rules Committee argued that to the black community this bill was an important symbol of national intent. Nothing else could dramatize so clearly whether America was prepared to go forward in the attempt to create, insofar as the law allowed, a free and open society where no citizen would be treated differently because of his creed, color, or national origin. One of the most persuasive supporters of the bill, Rep. William McCulloch of Ohio, the ranking Republican on the House Judiciary Committee, testified that every title of the bill would pass constitutional muster.

In the days before the vote I also read with care the Report of the National Advisory Commission on Civil Disorders, the Kerner Commission Report, which had been issued in early March. It warned that "our nation is moving toward two societies, one black, one white — separate and unequal." To me, its contents were stark and appalling. The report pointed out that in every single instance in 127 cities where racial incidents had taken place in the preceding two years, poor housing had been an important element in the total discontent of the black community.

Thirdly, the agonizing experiences of some of my own constituents helped convince me of the urgent necessity for action. I knew of a black schoolteacher in Rockford who not long before had answered some 100 advertisements looking for a home or apartment; she had been turned away in each and every case. I also knew of a young black engineer who had finally found a job commensurate with his educational background, then was forced to confess to me that he was leaving the community because he had not been able to find a suitable place for his family to live.

But beyond the witnesses in the Rules Committee, beyond the Kerner Commission Report, beyond the bitter experiences of some of my own constituents, there came to bear in my thinking the realization that as a Christian — as one who believes that God created all men in His own Image, and of one blood; and as one who believes that the Son of God brought His message of salvation without regard to race, color, or ethnic background — I had to be willing to give up age-old prejudices, even to the point of subordinating something as fundamental as the right of contract to the even more fundamental principle of human rights. After many moments of prayer, meditation, and careful consideration of my responsibility as a Christian, I concluded that I could do nothing less than cast my vote in support of legislation which was admittedly sweeping in its ramifications, but which seemed justified not only by the urgency of the hour, but by even more basic considerations of human rights and human dignity. By the weekend I had made up my mind to vote to send the Senate bill directly to the House floor, thus avoiding a Senate-House Conference.

Another factor now came into play. President Lyndon Johnson was scheduled to address a Joint Session of Congress on Monday night, the evening before the vote in the Rules Committee. Most observers expected him to endorse the Senate bill. I did not want it to appear that my vote on the bill was the result of Presidential pressure. Therefore, on Saturday afternoon I worked on a press release for the Sunday papers, stating my position. It said in part:

> . . . I believe that as a nation we must turn our face away from a course of segregation and separatism. We must re-affirm the essential human right to justice and human dignity. The Scriptures tell us that by our Christian faith we are become "agents of the reconciliation." Every American must be willing, in this dark and dangerous hour when angry voices seek to divide us and preach violence in our midst, to reject such counsels of despair. We must each of us resolve instead to become agents of reconciliation so that the wounds which now afflict us may be healed. Then and only then will a brighter day dawn for our beloved Country.

While I was working on the statement, a telephone call came from Richard Nixon, soon to become the party's standard bearer in the fall elections. He urged me to vote to bring the Senate bill to the floor right away. I thanked him for his call and told him I had already decided to do just that. His brief message of support was a welcome shot in the arm.

I was in my office working until after seven that evening. Driving home, as I pulled up onto Massachusetts Avenue from Rock Creek parkway, my car was stopped on the empty street by a young GI carrying a rifle. He demanded to know what I was doing out on the streets after

5

curfew. Only after identifying myself as a member of Congress and explaining that I had been in my office working late, could I proceed to drive home. This small incident made a profound impression on me. It made me realize that if something were not done soon to heal our national wounds, we might one day be forced to live and work in a garrisoned community.

As it happened, Martin Luther King was being buried in Atlanta when the Rules Committee convened for a vote on the Open Housing bill Tuesday morning. The committee chambers are on the third floor of the House wing of the Capitol, and that morning there were federal troops standing guard in the plaza just a stone's throw away. Rep. William Colmer, chairman of the committee and a Mississippi Democrat, pledged to oppose open housing, protested that we were "legislating under the gun." When the crucial vote came, I joined seven Democrats for an eight-to-seven majority against sending the Senate bill to Conference. A few minutes later the committee voted nine-to-six to send the bill to the House floor the next day, with provision for one hour of debate and no amendments.

That evening I sat at my desk at home until well past midnight preparing for the debate the next afternoon.

The House of Representatives convened as usual at twelve noon. Because the debate time was limited to one hour, only members of the two committees most responsible for the measure — Rules and Judiciary — were likely to be able to speak during the official debate. Other members of the House who wanted to go on record were taking the opportunity to make one-minute speeches before the first quorum call was issued, but as the second-ranking Republican on the Rules Committee, I felt reasonably assured of a chance to speak during the hour of official debate.

Rep. H. Allen Smith of California, senior Republican on the Rules Committee, was managing the "rule" on our side of the aisle. When I went over to the table to request a few minutes to speak, he informed me that he could not give me any time to present my views. Bitterly disappointed, and suspecting that he would have found time if my views had more closely approximated his own and those of the other Republicans on the committee, I walked away in a pique of resentment at the treatment I had received from a leader of my own party. A few moments later I managed to get recognition for a one-minute speech. There was time to express only a mere shadow of what I had wanted to say before the call was issued for a quorum of the House. I sat down, feeling that all my preparation of the night before had been in vain.

The debate began. Speaker John McCormack of Massachusetts warned the crowded galleries that clapping or other expressions of approval or disapproval were forbidden by House rule. Rep. Ray Madden of Indiana, a senior Democrat on the Rules Committee who was managing the floor debate for the majority, led off with a list of eminent citizens who had testified in favor of the Open Housing bill, from Attorney General Ramsey Clark to Mayor Ivan Allen of Atlanta. Next at the microphone in the well of the House Chamber was H. Allen Smith, speaking for those who opposed the bill.

On impulse, I walked over to where Rep. McCulloch was sitting. As senior Republican on the Judiciary Committee, I knew he would have some time to speak on the bill. I asked him if he would give me a few minutes of his own time. Bill McCulloch had been in the House of Representatives for twenty-two years; he had been speaking for equality under the law before I even knew what a bar exam was. Graciously, he let me have several precious minutes out of the five that had been given to him.

Rep. Joe Waggonner of Louisiana, a Democrat, was speaking now:

. . . I am sure the Members know that I know something about the Negro man — a good bit more about the Negro man than most of the Members do here — I have lived with them all my life, and I have more Negro friends than all of you put together, and the truth is the vast majority of the Negroes in this Country, at least ninety percent of them, are decent, law-abiding citizens, as is the case with the white people in this Country. But what is happening here today? We are ignoring that ninety percent of the white people and the Negro people who are decent, law-abiding citizens, and we of this Congress, you and I, are being blackmailed by that minority of ten percent.

So do not talk to me about the democratic process when we are being blackmailed as we are, and it is perfectly clear why: because these anarchists, these blackmailers, have been following the process of violence, blackmail, and threats, and believe that this Congress, day in and day out, will yield to their threats.

. . . It is crystal clear, gentlemen. There is no end to these demands. The next one will surely be a guaranteed annual wage, and, if we give in to this system of legislating by blackmail, what are you gentlemen going to do when the proposal is accompanied by more rioting, looting, and bloodshed? Give in again? Come back into this Chamber and say we have to rush this guaranteed annual wage bill through without even sending it to Committee or to Conference because the cities will be burned down if we do not? Is that what we are to reduce the legislative process to?

Well, not me. I want no part of it. We cannot react to blackmail in this manner.

Send this bill to Conference and give Conferees a chance to work out the bad parts, the unconstitutional parts, and let it come back for consideration when there is less tension in the air and without blackmail hanging over your heads.

He sat down. Rep. Smith yielded five minutes to Rep. McCulloch, who in turn yielded to me. Still smoldering from the earlier affront, I did not walk down the aisle and take the microphone in the well of the Chamber, but stood at one of the two committee tables which are positioned on either side of the aisle. I began:

Mr. Speaker, first let me thank the gentleman from Ohio for yielding. I want to pay him this tribute. I think his wisdom and his counsel in the matter of the splendid statement he made to the Committee on Rules on the constitutionality of this legislation was a very important factor so far as my own personal judgment on this matter is concerned.

I want to say that I think the violence that has stirred the soul and conscience of America during this past week has not blinded us to our responsibility here today. Rather, I would dare to hope that it has illumined that responsibility and has helped us to see, more clearly and more vividly than we otherwise would see, the responsibility that we have to try to translate into living reality the idea of equality of opportunity in housing . . . .

My wife and four-year-old daughter, Karen Beth were among those watching in the galleries. Suddenly Karen Beth turned to her mother and said, "That's not my daddy."

"Sure it is," my wife said.

"No, it's not," Karen Beth replied, "because he's angry."

. . . I think it would surprise you perhaps, if I said that I personally do not see this particular piece of legislation as any memorial to the dead. I see it rather as that cloud and that pillar that will guide the way of the living. In this open housing legislation we are not carving out any broad highway from the ghetto to the suburbs. At best it will be a narrow and tortuous road . . . .

I would respond to the gentleman from Louisiana by saying that those who have desecrated our Capital City during these past few days do not mourn the spirit of Martin Luther King. They are the excrescence of conditions that for all too long have been untended in our society.

In voting for this bill today, we do not vote to reward them — we vote rather to reward that ninety percent of whom he spoke — the decent, honest, and law-abiding citizens who would, if they could, relieve themselves of the bondage and escape the prison of the ghettos . . . .

In voting for this bill I seek to reward and encourage the millions of decent, hard-working, loyal, black Americans who do not riot and burn. I seek to give them the hope that the dream of owning a home in the suburbs or a decent apartment in the city will not be denied the man who was born black . . . .

Yes, I seek to reward those Negroes who can become responsible leaders of our society and diminish the influence of black racists and preachers of violence like Rap Brown and Stokeley Carmichael. If we would put out the fires of Negro revolution and defuse the social dynamite which has exploded in city after city across our land, we cannot separate the sane and sensible Negroes from the mainstream of American society. To do so is to encourage the eventual development of a garrison state where unbridled fear and suspicion rend us into two separate and unequal societies . . . .

I do not condone the rioting. Rather, I say, punish the violators of our laws. Let all men, black or white, understand that the religion of liberty is based on a reverence and respect for the law. But let us not be blind to the necessity of also rendering justice to the patient and the long-suffering who do not riot but who will be brought to the brink of despair if, like the priest and the Levite, we simply turn aside.

I would respectfully suggest to this House that we are not simply knuckling under to pressure or listening to the voices of unreasoning fear and hysteria if we seek to do that which we believe in our hearts is right and just. I legislate today not out of fear, but out of deep concern for the America I love.

We do stand at a crossroad. We can continue the Gadarene slide into an endless cycle of riot and disorder, or we can begin the slow and painful ascent toward that yet distant goal of equality of opportunity for all Americans regardless of race or color. Then perhaps we can dare hope, as John Addington Symonds wrote:

> "These things shall be — a loftier race
>   Than ere the world hath known shall rise,
> With flame of freedom in their souls
>   And light of knowledge in their eyes."

9

Paul tells us in his letter to the Hebrews that it was by faith that Abraham went forth to receive his inheritance, not knowing whither he went. That faith was the substance of things hoped for, the evidence of things not seen.

God grant us that faith in our destiny as a great nation — for Abraham Lincoln once described Americans as "God's almost chosen people." We cannot know how long the journey will take, or even precisely where it will take us, but with patience, with perseverance, and nobility of purpose, we can advance toward our goal of reconciliation and racial understanding.

I sat down, as *Newsweek* magazine later put it, "to a thunderous hand." But even more rewarding than the hand from the galleries was the hand offered by one of my colleagues in the House. Rep. John Conyers of Michigan, the young and highly respected leader of the Black Caucus, rose from his seat, crossed the aisle to the Republican side of the House, and grasped my hand in a display of feeling that the House rarely sees.

Within the hour the tally had been taken. The strong Open Housing bill passed the House of Representatives by a vote of 250 to 171. It went directly to the White House for signing and became the Civil Rights Act of 1968. The next day I was invited to witness the signing take place in the East Room of the White House. As I later passed through the Presidential reception line, the President clasped my hand warmly as one of his aides whispered to him that two days earlier in the Rules Committee it was my one vote that had truly made the difference.

2
ROCKFORD, ILLINOIS

"Dear Congressman: What made you decide to go into politics?"

School children especially like to ask that question, and I am not always sure whether it stems from a genuine desire to know, or from an assignment in civics. While it seems to me that a mass of biographical details would not be highly relevant to the purpose of this book, nor would much of it carry any great significance, I do believe that home and family, school and church, friends and counselors help to shape the career decisions that we ultimately make.

In 1922, when I was born in northwestern Illinois, the city of Rockford was a community of about 75,000 souls. Settled originally in the 1830's, its growth and development were greatly influenced by waves of immigration which brought thousands of Scandinavians to participate in the growing industry of the city in the 1880's and 1890's. Although Rockford was destined to become one of the largest producers of machine tools in the nation, its economy at the turn of the century and well into the 1920's rested on the furniture factories which offered employment to Swedish craftsmen attracted by the legendary opportunities America offered.

In 1901 my father, Albin Anderson, then only a fifteen-year-old boy, left the family farm in Westergotland, Sweden, to seek employment in one of these factories for a dollar a day. Accompanied only by an older sister, he made his way to the city that had become something of a Mecca for Swedish immigrants. Later his mother and father and three other sisters would all leave their native Sweden to establish a new home in America.

Strange as they found their adopted country to be in so many ways, there were certain comforting features. The southeast portion of the city, where they settled, was predominantly Swedish. There was a Swedish-American Bank and a Swedish-American Hospital. The language barrier did not seem so formidable when they could hear their native tongue spoken freely on one of the major shopping streets in this part of the city.

Father soon determined to become a merchant. He had courted and married Mabel Ring, the daughter of a Swedish immigrant who had a farm in the Stillman Valley area, some fifteen miles south of Rockford. For several years my parents operated a general store in the village of Stillman Valley. Then they moved to Rockford, where father began to operate a grocery store on Broadway, another shopping street in what was still a predominantly Scandinavian section of the city. In fact, the Swedes were so ubiquitous that they had to be known by some rather peculiar hyphenated names in order to distinguish the many Johnsons, Andersons, and Petersons. Thus there was "Coffee Johnson," and "Automobile Anderson," and "Shoeman Peterson."

Young Albin and Mabel Anderson began to raise a family. Three of their six children were to die early in childhood of scarlet fever and pneumonia. Perhaps because of this tragedy, the surviving children felt a close-knit relationship with their parents despite the long hours that father was absent tending his growing business. Some of my earliest memories are those of helping to stock the shelves, sweep the aisles, and do the other chores that made the after school hours and Saturdays fly.

If mother and dad had one verse of Scripture which represented the sum total of their child psychology, it was the familiar admonition of Proverbs 22:6, "Train up a child in the way he should go: and when he is old, he will not depart from it." They did not just rely on a puritan work ethic. They believed that outside of the home and school, time should be devoted to the church. That not only meant Sunday school at 9:29, rain or shine; it meant Sunday morning church service when a forty-five minute sermon was not considered unduly long, young peoples' service at five o'clock, and then a Sunday evening evangelistic service. It meant attendance at Wednesday night prayer meeting services, as well as the frequent "special meetings" which would bring well-known evangelists and Bible teachers to our city. It meant annual missionary conferences, where the cause of foreign missions would be laid upon the hearts of the people, usually by a recently returned missionary with slides of thatched huts in Africa, or patient water buffalo plodding along the rural byways of the Chinese interior.

In the summer, it meant visits to Camp Epworth, a religious campground where, in a tabernacle of somewhat rickety construction and uncertain vintage, we listened to Bible teachers and such scholars as the late Professor Widell and Dr. Harry Lindbloom. Then during the sultry "dog days" of August, on the school grounds of one of the East

Side elementary schools, five of the East Side Scandinavian churches of evangelical persuasion would hold a "Union Tent Campaign." There was as yet no air conditioning, and the tent meetings meant an escape from the stuffy interiors which became stifling on hot summer nights. It was also a time when a noted evangelist would be called to conduct a soul-winning crusade.

It was in one of these meetings, when I was just a child of nine, that I felt so moved by the message being preached that I made a public confession of my desire to accept the Lord Jesus Christ as my personal Savior. Many years later, when I was asked to describe this event in my life, I did so in these words (this account appeared in the *Evangelical Beacon*):

> It was a warm summer Sunday evening in August. Dr. Paul Rood was the evangelist that year at what used to be the annual tent meeting campaign sponsored by five of Rockford's East Side Swedish Churches. Seated there beside my parents on the rough planking of a make-shift church pew, I was suddenly gripped as never before in my young life by the message of this divinely-gifted man of God.
>
> His text was the old, yet ever-new message of John 3:16. Those words: "Ye must be born again" still reecho in my ears just as they did on the warm, still air of that evening long ago. Those of you who were privileged to hear Dr. Rood, know the passionate intensity with which he spoke. On that night, the Word of God as he expounded it simply and clearly became the "Sword of the Spirit" that pierced my heart and convicted me of my complete unworthiness. There under the canvas of what had once been the "Big Top" of one of those innumerable little circuses that toured the country but have now become as sanctified as any great cathedral, I fell on my knees and beseeched God's mercy.
>
> I can also remember the words that I used when Dr. Rood asked those of us who had truly been born again to publicly confess our faith. When my turn to testify came, I simply said, "I know that He knows that I know Him." Even as I write these words, I cannot help but marvel at the clarity of these details in my mind as I recall that truly glorious experience. The really important thing, of course, is not the particularity with which I recall those sacred moments of intro-spection and conversion. Rather, it is that I have the assurance that by this event I was reconciled to God. I have the precious knowledge that the instant of my salvation was not one of those ephemeral events that partake of such rapture at the moment and then slowly but in-evitably fade into the oblivion of man's forgetfulness. I remember not just a simple sequence of events related in time, but the cataclysmic change that is eternal in its consequence.

13

For me personally, the recollection of the night of my rebirth does far more than provoke a nostalgia for the carefree days of childhood. It serves as a constant reminder of the miracle of regeneration. It provides the assurance that the same Christ who could touch the heart of a child is also sufficient unto all of my needs today.

I have never been ashamed to recount that experience, because I am absolutely convinced that God's transforming love can change the heart of a child or an adult. I can say with the apostle Paul, "For I am not ashamed of the gospel of Christ: for it is the power of God unto salvation to every one that believeth; to the Jew first, and also to the Greek" (Romans 1:16).

The cynic and the sophisticate will perhaps dismiss a religious conversion as the product of overwrought emotions which have been fanned by fears of eternal damnation or the hope of some euphoric future existence. There are "conversions" of that genre, make no mistake about it. Our Lord tells us as much, I believe, in His parable of the sower who went forth to sow, when some of his seed fell upon a rock where it took root and then withered away because it lacked moisture (Luke 8:6). However, I believe that for every ephemeral conversion there are many others which do represent the kind of experience the apostle Paul describes in II Corinthians 5:17, "Therefore if any man be in Christ, he is a new creature: old things are passed away; behold, all things are become new."

I do believe that if a child receives religious training in his own home, the chances of a religious conversion being the kind of meaningful experience that leads to a long-term commitment to Christ are greatly enhanced. This is not to disparage the authenticity of those decisions for Christ which occur so spontaneously and in such great numbers under the ministry of a great evangelist like Billy Graham. But I think there is a relevant analogy between a decision reinforced by Christian training and those desert plants which can withstand the prolonged broiling rays of the desert sun because within their cells have been stored the vital drops of moisture which enable them to survive. New Christians who have been able to store the warmth and love generated by a Christian family have received something that can sustain their nascent faith against the desert winds of doubt and adversity.

In the great debate over an integrated society which has taken place in recent years, we have had fresh evidence in such widely accepted sociological documents as the Coleman Report that the influence of home and family life on a child's educational program and development is of critical importance. I am convinced that what is true in a secular sense has a certain validity in the spiritual dimension of our lives. What a responsibility this imposes on us as parents to provide an atmosphere of Christian love and understanding within the bosom of our family! Then as our children grow and develop, they can store up the water of spiritual knowledge to refresh and sustain the seed that may later fall upon their hearts under the converting power of the Holy Spirit.

When I entered the University of Illinois in 1939, I was still uncertain as to the choice of a career. In high school, my chief claim to fame had been my ability as a debater and winner of speech contests. This aptitude, coupled with a decision to major in political science, led me to gravitate toward law school. My legal education was interrupted for a two-and-a-half-year stint in the field artillery in Europe during World War Two. Following the war, I returned to the University of Illinois Law School, where I received my law degree of Juris Doctor (J.D.) in 1946.

I returned to Rockford to practice with one of the larger law firms. One of the senior partners had heard me debate before a Lions Club luncheon some years earlier and had been sufficiently impressed to offer me a job upon graduation, largely on the strength of that performance. For two years I tried cases in the Justice of the Peace Court, did legal research, examined abstracts of title, wrote collection letters, and did the other things that fledgling lawyers customarily do during their apprenticeship.

However, I was still searching for some larger satisfaction, and when the opportunity for a graduate fellowship to Harvard Law School presented itself, I promptly headed for Cambridge, Massachusetts. The year of graduate study under men like the late Henry Hart and the great Paul Freund was an exhilarating one. It occurred to me that I would perhaps like to teach, and indeed for a short time while attending classes at Harvard, I was a part-time instructor at what was then the Northeastern University School of Law in Boston. However, the teaching offers were not particularly attractive financially, so I returned to Rockford and the practice of law.

In 1952 another wave of restlessness seized me, and I elected to join the Foreign Service and become a diplomat. After a rigorous two-and-a-half-day written exam in Chicago, which impressed me as being tougher than my bar exam a few years earlier, I went to Washington, where I successfully passed an oral examination given by a Board of Senior Foreign Service Officers. In July I began my ninety-day Foreign Service Officer's basic training course, prior to being assigned to serve with the State Department abroad.

About midway through the course we were instruced to complete all of the formalities required for the issuance of our diplomatic passports. This included going to the Walker Johnson Building in Washington to have a passport photo taken. The young lady who took my picture was a striking brunette with the unusual name of Keke. Alas, the first photograph proved entirely unsuitable; I had closed my eyes as she clicked the shutter. I have since told my wife that this was one deal that I didn't go into with my eyes open, because I returned with alacrity for a new photo, and a new chapter in my life began.

The chance meeting developed into an acquaintanceship that lasted during the remaining weeks I was in Washington. We climbed the hills of Rock Creek Park together, dined by candlelight in the innumerable little restaurants for which the National Capital is famous, and I soon realized that I had fallen in love. If any proof was needed of the old adage that absence makes the heart grow fonder, a few weeks at my first post abroad in West Berlin, Germany, dispelled my doubts. I cabled Keke to come to Germany, and on 4 January 1953, we were married at St. Anne's Lutheran Church, the oldest Protestant church in Berlin, dating back to the fourteenth century.

Those were fascinating years in Germany. In 1953, the first full year that I was in West Berlin, more than 300,000 East Germans fled to freedom. The infamous wall was still eight years from being built, and they simply took the underground or U-Bahn in the Soviet Sector of East Berlin and made their way to freedom in the West. I interviewed scores of them in connection with my work when I visited the refugee camps in the city. Their stories of political persecution were a vivid corroboration of the barrenness of life under a Communist dictatorship. Walter Ulbricht, or Der Spitzbart as they called him (because of his pointed goatee), seemed as ruthless as Stalin in his extirpation of personal liberties.

I left Germany in 1955 when my tour was over. I had decided to resign and return to the practice of law. It was a difficult decision, as life in the Foreign Service had been both stimulating and exciting. However, I chafed under what seemed to me the paramilitary organization and structure of the Foreign Service. There were economic considerations too. Our first child, Eleanora, was born in January of 1954, and the $5,093.00 salary of a Junior Officer often seemed inadequate. Perhaps the greatest consideration was the inchoate feeling that somewhere there might be broader horizons and greater possibilities for personal advancement than within the rather rigid structure of the Foreign Service.

And so with my young bride and year-old child, I returned to the United States and a somewhat less than certain future. Twice I had forsaken the practice of law to attempt something quite outside the confines of that profession, and now I was returning to it again.

I suppose that by this extremely circuitous route, I have come to the point of trying to answer that very elusive question, "Congressman, how did you get into politics?" After only a year back in Rockford, I found myself, in the spring of 1956, engaged in a hard-fought, five-man race for the Republican nomination for the office of State's Attorney. In Illinois the State's Attorney is the chief criminal prosecutor for the county; he also serves as counsel to the County Board of Supervisors and handles civil litigation for the county. It was a job for a lawyer, and I was a lawyer.

There were other reasons for my decision. Having newly reestablished my practice, and being barred by the canons of ethics from advertising for clients, the campaign provided, win or lose, an excellent means of putting my name and qualifications before the public. I also had encouragement from close friends. Some were undoubtedly interested in me as an individual; others with a more calculated view thought it would be advantageous for the Party to offer a fresh young face. I was blessed with no apocalyptic vision of bringing better government to an oppressed people. Basically, I entered politics because I felt that a career in public life and public service offered me the possibility of greater personal satisfaction than the continued private practice of law.

I prayed over this initial decision to seek public office, just as I have prayed over every major decision in my life. I do not believe we can expect God to insure our success at the polls. God's help may indeed prove to be the decisive element, but it is not given simply to gratify our human desire for victory over our opponents. But we can ask God to give us the assurance of His presence by our side in the political arena. We can pray as Solomon did: "Give therefore thy servant an understanding heart to judge thy people, that I may discern between good and bad . . ." (I Kings 3:9). The prescription today for good government is what it was three thousand years ago. We need legislators, judges, and administrators who recognize that it is God who bestows the wisdom, understanding, and largeness of heart to interpret His truth and justice among men.

As it happened, I was elected State's Attorney of Winnebago County and thus took the first step toward a career in public office. Then in 1959, while I was in the third year of my elected term, the incumbent Congressman from the District announced his plans to retire. After fourteen terms in Washington, he had become so strongly entrenched that rarely, if ever, did he encounter serious opposition in his campaign for reelection. I did not think seriously about running for the vacant seat until one of my close friends suggested it. By this time a veteran State Senator had already jumped into the race and there were rumblings from several other potential candidates. As is often the case when an office has been held for many years by the same man, the wings are crowded with those waiting to come on stage.

The decision to enter what promised to be a difficult and hard-fought contest was not easy. I prayerfully considered what the future might hold. Although I had enjoyed the experience of being State's Attorney and the knowledge it had brought me of problems in the field of law enforcement, I did not intend to seek another term. I had no desire to make a career out of being a criminal prosecutor and felt that a return to private practice offered greater advantages. I was attracted by the challenge of a position where I would be considering national issues as well as those dealing with American foreign relations.

By the time I actually entered the race, four other candidates had thrown their hats into the ring. The critical hurdle was the Republican primary election which would be held in April. The State Senator from a neighboring county was reputed to be in the lead for the nomination. However, out of the field of five I was the best known in my home county, the most populous of the seven counties in northwestern Illinois which made up the 16th Congressional District. Therefore, my co-workers and I concentrated our most strenuous efforts on getting precinct and block workers in the city of Rockford, and carefully built an effective grass-roots organization.

I also purchased a small Rambler station wagon and had it repainted in bright colors with my name blazoned on both sides. Loading it with boxes of campaign materials, brochures, buttons, matchbooks, and other paraphernalia, I sallied forth to get acquainted in the numerous small towns and in the countryside where my name was far from being a household word. I attended livestock auctions and sometimes succeeded in getting the auctioneer to give me three minutes "in the ring" to harangue the audience of farmers who were somewhat impatiently waiting for the bidding to resume. But I persevered, and every now and then it seemed to me I caught a glimmer of interest.

The list of functions at which people got together was endless. There were parades, festivals, pancake suppers, spaghetti suppers, church ice cream socials, Rotary and Kiwanis Club luncheons. If I could make a speech, fine. Otherwise, I did my best to smile, shake hands, and project an image of sincere determination. Oftentimes I would simply pick a street corner or a shopping center and advance on startled or bemused passers-by with a cheery, "Hi, I'm John Anderson. I'm running for Congress, and I'd sure appreciate your vote."

My wife joined in the effort. Often she would be in one area of the Congressional District while I was campaigning somewhere else. I later learned that many people were so impressed with her that they were willing to vote for her husband sight unseen. She used to tease me by saying that if she had been a candidate herself she might have defeated all five men who were running.

The day of the primary election in April finally came. We were close to physical exhaustion after months of day and night campaigning. I have always believed that American political campaigns, even on a Congressional level, are too long and too expensive. That evening after the polls closed, we repaired to our storefront headquarters, which had been provisioned with gallons of coffee (as if I had not already attended scores of coffee parties and drunk hundreds of cups during the campaign) and boxes of doughnuts. There was a victory cake, but it had to remain carefully out of sight during the early part of the evening.

Finally, the first returns came in from the city. It showed me carrying some of the East Side wards, where I had grown up, by margins of four to one and five to one. As the news trickled in more slowly from distant counties, we found that in two of them I had virtually tied my principal opponent. In others I did more poorly, but the huge margin in my hometown was decisive. By ten o'clock that evening, I knew that I had won the crucial Republican primary. I went on to win the November election without difficulty, and a new chapter in my life had begun.

3
THE NATION'S CAPITAL: EYEWITNESS TO HISTORY

In January, 1961, I returned to the nation's capital, where I had signed on as a Junior Foreign Service Officer eight years before. I had to ask a Capitol policeman, with some embarrassment, how to find my office. As a freshman I had been assigned to small and wholly unpretentious quarters on the second floor of Longworth, one of three office buildings across the street from the House Chamber.

It mattered not, for I moved as if in a dream through those first few weeks. It was enough that I was strolling the halls of the Capitol where Henry Clay, Daniel Webster, and other Congressional greats had walked. There was no orientation course for freshman Congressmen. Like the other newcomers, I respectfully inquired of my elders as to what the procedures were both on and off the Floor, and somehow muddled through those first months of the 87th Congress.

To the casual and unpracticed eye the House often seems a model of egalitarian democracy, where one vote counts the same as any other and the Representative of each Congressional district is given an equal voice in shaping the nation's laws. In fact, it just isn't so, and the informed observer of House politics and procedures knows that some votes and some voices count for a great deal more than others.

Power in the House is tightly governed by a time-honored, age-encrusted organizational structure, of which the two chief components are the Committee System and the Seniority System. The subsequent career in the House of any incoming Representative is greatly influenced, if not determined, by the way in which these two systems work. Thus it may be worth taking a moment to describe them.

Many people have the impression that the important business of the House is conducted on the floor of the great Chamber in the Capitol, scene of many an impassioned debate and cliff-hanging vote. But the more serious work actually goes on in the twenty-one Standing Committees of the House. No significant piece of legislation ever gets to the

House floor without being laboriously screened and shaped by one of the committees, such as Agriculture, Armed Services, Banking and Currency, Foreign Affairs, or Judiciary. Once a bill does get to the House Floor, only rarely is the judgment of its parent committee overturned by a vote of the full House. Thus committee assignments are crucial, not just to the individual freshman Representative who must make his mark as a legislator by conscientiously doing his committee homework, but to the overall impact of the House on the great and growing body of federal law.

Obviously it is a great boost to the aspirations of a new Congressman if he can win appointment by his party's leadership either to one of the more prestigious committees, or to one in which his training, expertise, and interest will allow him to make an early mark. Of the twenty-one House Committees, three are generally regarded as being of special importance: the Ways and Means Committee, which exercises the prerogative of the House to originate tax bills in the Congress; the Appropriations Committee, which monitors all money bills; and the Rules Committee, which as we have seen decides when and under what conditions important bills will come to the House Floor. But a young Congressman might also have a particular reason for wanting to go on the Interstate and Foreign Commerce Committee, for example, and thus he may request the leadership to nominate him for a spot there. If for some reason he has incurred the displeasure of the powers that be, then he may be denied the choice committee assignments he desires. The most conspicuously cited example in recent years was the failure of New York's John Lindsay to win a post on the House Foreign Affairs Committee while he was serving in the House of Representatives.

Once on a committee, a Congressman's advancement is rigidly governed by the Seniority System, according to which those members of the majority party who have the longest tenure in Congress are awarded the chairmanships of their respective committees. This means that virtually all real power is concentrated in the hands of very senior members. We will have more to say about the Seniority System in a later chapter, but suffice it to say that for a young incoming Congressman, the Committee System and Seniority System loom as fascinating but forbidding mechanisms for wielding power in the House.

I was somewhat disappointed by my original assignment to the House Committees on Administration and Government Operations. The former is the housekeeping committee of the House of Representatives, regarded as a minor committee charged with authorizing funds to equip and staff the House and its twenty-one Standing Committees. The Government Operations Committee plays an investigative role, and in recent years has likewise been regarded as a minor rather than major repository of power in the House.

However, I was counseled to be patient, with the understanding that in succeeding terms I could improve my committee status. This did occur, although not until I suffered another disappointment in being denied a vacancy on the Ways and Means Committee, when a colleague from Illinois with considerably more seniority decided to assert his prerogative of transfer, although he was already serving on another major committee at the time. I suffered this disappointing failure to secure a post on the Ways and Means Committee with sufficient good grace to commend me to the House Leadership for another important committee. Thus largely as a consolation prize, the Minority Leader arranged to give me an appointment to the Joint Committee on Atomic Energy. This committee enjoys great prestige because it monitors both the military and civilian atomic energy programs, which range from warheads for our ICBM's to such peaceful applications as the generation of electric power in plants which use atomic fuel and experiments designed to stimulate the production of natural gas.

Less than a year after my selection for the Atomic Energy Committee, a member of the important House Rules Committee resigned his seat. As we saw in Chapter One, this committee's position astride the legislative pathway can on occasion give it decisive power over an important bill. I launched a campaign to win a seat on the Rules Committee, which required contacting each member of the Committee on Committees. These members cast a weighted vote, depending on the size of their state delegations, when choices are made to fill a vacancy. This meant that states like Illinois, Ohio, Michigan, California, and Pennsylvania — states with sizeable Republican House delegations — carry the most weight. The ranking Republican on the Rules Committee was Clarence Brown of Ohio, since deceased. He seemed to have some regard for me, which dated back to our service together on the Government Operations Committee. Also weighing in my favor was the notion that this was an "Illinois seat" on the Rules Committee, since an Illinoisan had occupied it for twenty-eight years. Brown's help and that of my own Illinois delegation gave me powerful allies, and in the end I was appointed to the vacant Rules seat.

For the first eight years of my tenure in the House, I served as a member of the opposition party, a Republican under Democratic presidents. They were eventful, at times agonizing, but always challenging years. Nevertheless, you can imagine the mounting sense of excitement that members of our party felt as Richard Nixon carried the Presidency and began to form a Republican Administration in the last months of 1968. A new era was beginning in Washington, an era that many of us had looked toward and patiently labored for since we had first come to Congress. What was not immediately apparent was that this new era would also open a new and challenging opportunity for me personally, within the party organization in the House of Representatives.

In December, 1968, President-elect Nixon named Rep. Melvin Laird of Wisconsin to be Secretary of Defense in his new Cabinet. As Chairman of the House Republican Conference, Laird had been the third ranking Republican in the House and a very effective member of the G.O.P. Congressional leadership. His move to the Defense Department left the Conference Chairmanship vacant.

Several other highly-respected members of our party in the House coveted the job, but I was urged by some of my friends to consider making a try for it. I had good relations with most of my House Republican colleagues, and my open housing speech in April of 1968 had caused some attention to come my way. But the decision was a serious one, as it would involve campaigning for a post with considerable responsibility and influence, and some power, in the House Republican leadership. On this, as on other occasions, I sought the advice of friends and spent much time in prayer over whether this would be an appropriate and wise move to make.

Ironically, just before the announcement of Melvin Laird's appointment was made, I had finally decided against joining some of my colleagues on a trip to Latin America. If I had gone, there would have been no chance to mount a campaign for the Conference Chairmanship, and the job would doubtless have fallen to another worthy aspirant.

After due consideration of my chances and the responsibility involved, I decided to make the try. Much of the actual behind-the-scenes work was done by friends who supported my candidacy. Rep. Jim Harvey of Michigan and his staff were especially helpful, and there were friends from Illinois and other delegations who helped marshal the needed votes.

There were 187 Republican members of the House, and I would need a simple majority to win.

I spent the days before the first Republican Conference meeting of the new session in January on the phone, talking to as many members as possible and asking for their support. We also sent telegrams to each member on the day of the vote, urging them to vote for John Anderson for Chairman. Many had already pledged their support, and I was confident that I stood a good chance of being elected when the vote came.

Then in the last forty-eight hours before the vote, dissent surfaced in the Ohio delegation. Ohio had by far the largest Republican delegation of any state, and yet the way things were going they would have no real voice in the party's House leadership. There was already one Illinoisan, Rep. Leslie Arends, in the leadership; as Whip, he was second in line behind the Minority Leader. I had announced for the number three position, the Conference Chairmanship, and yet another Illinoisan, Donald Rumsfeld, had thrown his hat into the ring for the Chairmanship of the Research Committee, another important leadership post. To offset this "imbalance," many members of the Ohio delegation wanted one of their own in the leadership, and they chose Rep. Jackson Betts, a senior member of their own delegation, as their candidate for the Conference Chairmanship.

When the Conference met early in January, Rep. Gerald Ford of Michigan was nominated and elected as Republican candidate for Speaker of the House without opposition. Since we were the Minority Party, he would become the Minority Leader. Les Arends was then confirmed as Whip. I was elected Conference Chairman by a gratifying total of 117 votes against 50 for my nearest rival, and Rep. Robert Taft of Ohio was elected Chairman of the Research Committee.

The Conference Chairmanship added a new dimension to my work as a Congressman. The Conference itself is the body of all Republicans who serve in the House of Representatives. We meet periodically to discuss important pending legislation and have the power to adopt resolutions in the name of House Republicans, as we did in November of 1969, expressing support for the president's policy of phased withdrawal in Vietnam. The Chairman of the Conference is invited to attend the weekly Republican Congressional Leadership meetings in the Cabinet Room of the White House, attended by the President and the Vice-President. In addition to a discussion of legislative strategy, these sessions provide an extremely valuable forum for the President to personally brief his legislative leaders in the House and Senate on his plans and policies. They also provide an insight, and in many cases a preview, into the manner in which the President engages in battle on a complex problem or controversial issue.

I am often asked: "What is the real allure of life in Washington?" Perhaps for some the attraction is the beauty of the city (although in the excessively humid days of July and August, there are those who grumble that the idea of a summer Capital elsewhere ought to be more agressively explored). For others it may be a hyper-active social life, embassy parties, White House receptions and musicales for the favored few, and a constant round of official and private functions. Then there are always those who gravitate to the seats of power, be they social, economic, or political, seeking whatever advantage may come their way. These are the political camp followers and the others who live by their wits or the influence, sometimes real but often fancied, which they pretend to command.

However, in my judgment, these are all superficialities. The immense satisfaction that comes to me from being a part of the Washington scene is the daily knowledge that, as a member of the world's greatest parliamentary body, I am at the very center of the decision-making process on matters of enormous consequence to the nation, and indeed, oftentimes the entire world. There is a certain mystique about being an eyewitness to history. This book opened with a fairly detailed description of the events which led up to the single most decisive vote which I have cast during my years in the Congress. During those years there have been literally hundreds of other votes, which, although lacking in similar climactic impact, have helped to fashion the history of our times.

And so, throughout the turbulent and sometimes tragic decade of the Sixties, I feel that I have been specially privileged to be in Washington, the almost literal nerve center of the world, as an observer and participant in great historical events. I also believe deeply that I have been where God wanted me to be. The late Adlai Stevenson once told the story of the youngster whose father had just been elected to Congress. That night as she knelt by her bed to say her prayers, her parents were dismayed to hear her say, as she finished repeating, "Now I lay me down to sleep" . . . the words, "And now, it's goodbye, God. Tomorrow we're all moving to Washington." In perhaps the most secular environment in the world, I believe God can be and is present in the lives of many men who share the responsibility for making, interpreting, and administering our nation's laws.

As I look back on this decade in Congress, I am conscious of an evolutionary change and development in my attitudes on some important issues. The impact of the Kennedy assassination and the turbulence of the years that followed have certainly influenced my attitudes on such questions as civil rights and the role of the federal government in fighting poverty and attacking urban problems. The agonizing futility of the war in Vietnam, about which I will have more to say later, has likewise stimulated a belief that if we would only work half as hard on initiatives for peace as we do on developing sophisticated new weaponry, our chances for survival on this planet would be greater than they are.

After serving for ten years in the fastest-moving, most pivotal spot on earth, it would be difficult to remain completely immune to the forces of change that have been unleashed in the past few years. New technology, new research and ideas in every sphere of human activity, literally ricochet through the chamber of our minds as we are catapulted ahead by the explosion of human knowledge. Inevitably there are those who watch with hawkish eye for any deviation from a pattern of thinking and voting which they regard as an immutable constitutional norm. They might, for example, regard a vote to include the so-called working poor in a reform of the nation's welfare system as a subsidy to the indolent. Possibly they would not go as far as Senator Long of Louisiana and refer to mothers receiving aid to dependent children as "brood mares," but they would perhaps smile at the suggestion. There was a time when I might have voted against the president's welfare reform proposal as an incentive to laziness, but I have come to feel that I can no longer avert my eye from this problem and with Pharisaical mien thank the Lord that I am not as other men.

Similarly, on the question of extending the right to vote to eighteen-year-olds, some refuse to accept the argument that today we have a generation which, by virtue of education and exposure to the world and all its problems, is more politically sophisticated and socially aware than any other in our history. They marry, raise families, work, pay taxes, go off to war at eighteen, nineteen, and twenty, and therefore understandably seek some voice in the decisions which will affect them during the balance of their lives. I cite this latter example especially because ten years ago I doubt very much that I would have supported this proposition. Now I believe that the very survival of our system of representative government depends on a willingness to make the adaptations and accept the changed circumstances that require us to strike out boldly in new directions as we continue our journey into the final third of this century. American democracy must not become a stagnant pool. Rather it must continue to be a rushing stream that, while canalized between the boundaries of our fundamental law, the Constitution, can move swiftly enough to carry the commerce of new ideas and new endeavors toward the goal of a more just, more open society for all our people.

Let me conclude this chapter by emphasizing the conviction that this decade of political and social transformation has also made it abundantly clear to me that we desperately need Divine guidance as we make our decisions here in Washington. Some theologians have referred to this as the "Post-Christian age." It is undeniably one of the most secular ages in human history. Even the church in some instances has sought to accommodate its teachings to a belief that secular values are paramount to spiritual values.

Yet how foolish we would be, and with what tragic consequences, if we left the bedrock of our spiritual traditions at this turbulent, trying time in our nation's history. On a recent visit to Israel I had occasion to fly over the historic spot where Moses received the law. As our plane slowly circled Mt. Sinai, a rugged peak jutting up from the desert floor, I was overwhelmed again with the realization that our Judaeo-Christian heritage is the very foundation on which society in the Western World rests. Take away this base, and the whole structure will crumble.

Exodus 19:20 says, "And the Lord came down upon mount Sinai, on the top of the mount: and the Lord called Moses *up* to the top of the mount; and Moses went up." I believe that if men in government at any level of administration — national, state, or local — are going to have any chance of success in dealing with today's problems, they must begin by looking up. We need to rediscover the book of God's law, as did Josiah of old, and experience as he did a spiritual reformation, if we are going to contend with the forces of darkness in our day. Whether it is drug abuse among teen-agers, the soaring crime rate in our cities, or unrest on college campuses, we need to see the spiritual dimension of these problems. Then as the scales of blindness fall from our eyes, and we are moved by Divine love and compassion, we may yet find the solutions that seem to elude us today.

I believe the challenge can be met. And with God's help, I hope to continue to play a small part in the unfolding drama of our times.

4
A
WEEK
IN
THE
LIFE

What is the life of a Congressman actually like? Sometimes it is hard to get an accurate picture, because press coverage so often centers on crucial votes, debates, and committee hearings. Sometimes the impression is given that we spend most of our time being entertained and importuned by lobbyists, or indulging ourselves in political infighting in smoke-filled caucus rooms.

All of these are part of the picture, but to offer a more realistic perspective, let me describe how I actually spent one week in the fall of 1969, the week of the first Vietnam Moratorium, October 12-18.

Sunday

I spent the weekend at home in Illinois' 16th District. Sunday morning there was a dedication ceremony for a new Christian education building at the First Baptist Church in Rockford, and in the afternoon two more meetings in rural towns. Then I drove to Savanna on the Mississippi River and gave a talk before a Methodist men's group. I arrived back at Washington's Dulles Airport well after midnight.

Monday

By nine o'clock I was in my office in the Longworth Building, just across the street from the Capitol, answering mail by dictation, going through a stack of letters on my desk, and talking with my aides about projects for the week, including whether or not I should go to Elmhurst (Illinois) College to speak to a campus meeting on Moratorium Day.

At 10:30, I attended a meeting with Vice President Agnew on the Senate side of the Capitol, along with other Congressmen and Senators who were hoping to get some indication of Administration support for a consolidation of federal programs in maritime research and development, through the establishment of a proposed National Oceanic and Atmospheric Agency.

The House met at noon and heard President Nixon's message to Congress on the Administration's new legislative proposals. Some other members of the House Republican Leadership and I made brief remarks in support of the President's program. It was a short session, otherwise devoted to District of Columbia and private bills; we adjourned at two o'clock.

Most of the afternoon I spent in the office, working on remarks for the debate on the postal pay raise bill coming up the next day. There were more letters to be answered and signed. On a typical day such as this, much time is spent taking telephone calls from constituents in the 16th District and from other Congressmen concerned about upcoming legislation. There were also calls from a couple of journalists who wanted to know how I felt about the Vietnam Moratorium. I left about 6:30 for a quiet evening at home with my wife, Keke, and our children: Eleanora, 16; John, Jr., 13; Diane, 11, and Karen, 6.

Tuesday

At 8:30 A.M., I was at the White House for the weekly Republican Congressional Leadership breakfast, which lasted two hours. President Nixon chose this occasion to explain his position on the appointment of Judge Clement Haynsworth to the Supreme Court and to get the reactions of Republican Congressional leaders.

I was in a bind that morning because of conflicting meetings, both of them important. The House Rules Committee normally meets at 10:30 on Tuesdays, and I was very interested in the morning's agenda, the Housing and Urban Development Act of 1969, for I intended to offer an amendment once the bill reached the floor.

However, I had to give that meeting short shrift because of an important meeting of the House Republican Conference, which I chair. The Conference overwhelmingly voted a resolution of support for President Nixon's Vietnam policy and then briefly discussed the postal pay raise bill coming up on the floor that afternoon.

After the conference meeting, I held a press conference in the Speaker's Lobby and tried to explain the intent of our Vietnam resolution and my own views on the Moratorium. I also answered questions about what was discussed at the White House Leadership breakfast.

The House met at noon as usual. I waited my turn to make a short speech on the Moratorium, which is included here because it is typical

29

of the kind of speeches made by Members before the House is called to consider the important pending legislation for the day:

MR. ANDERSON of Illinois. Mr. Speaker, over the past few weeks we have seen growing public interest in the administration's efforts to end the Vietnam war. We have seen legitimate and constructive discussion by the young as well as the old, by the "outs" as well as the "ins." In the current debate the Vietnam Moratorium Committee has played a particularly active part in encouraging discussion of the U.S. role in Vietnam. I think this debate is healthy. I agree with Congressman Rogers Morton that this kind of responsible discussion is a good thing for our country. However, I want to ask a few hard questions this morning because I have been disappointed by the public discussion to date — and I hope that we can make tomorrow's day of debate more constructive by trying to focus on realistic alternatives, which I sometimes feel have been forgotten in the atmosphere of excitement that has been growing over the past few weeks.

First of all I wonder — and I specifically want to ask those Senators and Congressmen who have endorsed the moratorium tomorrow — if an adequate distinction has been made between the objective of the moratorium and the means that are being used to achieve that objective. The means that are to be used — public discussions, peaceful marches, and organized campaigns to encourage American citizens to express their feelings about the war and the direction of U.S. policy — are all in the best traditions of American freedom of thought, speech, and assembly. It would be a travesty on American history if any political leader suggested that U.S. citizens did not have this right, or ought not to exercise it. I would only add that I firmly and sincerely hope that this day of debate will be a peaceful one, for if it is not, irreparable harm may be done to these most precious of our freedoms.

So I say that the means are legitimate, but I have grave questions about the stated goal of the moratorium leaders. And I further suspect that the many statements of support or opposition by public figures in the past few days may have done more to confuse than to clarify that goal in the public mind. Yesterday I asked the moratorium organizers for a formal statement of their objectives. Mr. David Mixner, one of the committee leaders, gave this reply:

"We want to show that it is politically possible and desirable to support complete, immediate, and unilateral withdrawal. We want out now, and this is not contingent on anything that Hanoi or the Viet Cong might do."

Do Senators Muskie, Kennedy, McGovern, and others who have endorsed the moratorium also support this objective? If not, then in the interest of more responsible debate on a question of critical importance to the nation, I would ask them to make clear just where they do stand — not only on the general question of public discussion of the issues — in which I fully agree with them — but also on the specific question of immediate and unilateral withdrawal as a goal of U.S. policy in Vietnam.

Second, I would like to make clear again, in case some have forgotten already, that the announced policy of the Nixon administration is to end the Vietnam war as quickly and honorably as possible. There is broad agreement on this policy — much broader, I submit, than on the moratorium objective of immediate, unilateral withdrawal. It is clear that this war has become the concern of all Americans. I think an overwhelming majority of our people want this war brought to an early and honorable end. That is one reason Richard Nixon was elected President in November, because he recognized that widespread feeling throughout the nation. I hope that tomorrow Americans will remember that the President has already taken important steps to reduce our own role in the fighting, to encourage the South Vietnamese to shoulder more of their own burden, and to bring about a reduced level of hostilities in Vietnam at the same time that he is actively seeking an early end to the war in Paris.

Finally, I ask myself, and I would like the American people to ask themselves, whether the atmosphere of excitement and emotional commitment that has prevailed in the past few days, and will reach its peak tomorrow, is the kind of atmosphere in which major decisions affecting a critical national policy should be made. I do not say this policy should not be reviewed. I do not suggest that important decisions should not be made — decisions which may affect the size and scope and schedule of our commitment in South Vietnam. I only suggest that a time of high excitement and emotional response is not the time when grave national decisions ought to be made. These important decisions ought to be made carefully and quietly, after serious reflection, in an atmosphere of studied deliberation. Let us express ourselves as a people — or more accurately, let us express ourselves as groups of people. But let us do it carefully, responsibly, peacefully, as befits a democratic nation which understands that great questions of war and peace are solved neither by sloganeering, nor by public posturing, nor even by dramatic days of debate and dissent.

I do not ask, and I do not think the President asks, for the kind of strict unity behind a person or policy that would silence dissent or imply that it is un-American. The right to disagree, and to disagree publicly along with others of the same persuasion, is one of our most precious freedoms. I hope and believe that what we will see tomorrow will be a positive, peaceful reaffirmation of that right. But let us also remember that the cause of peace is not served simply by strident voices rising in concert. As the Washington Post recently observed:

"A loud shout to stop the war, however heartfelt, is not a strategy."

Mr. Speaker, the President too seeks peace and disengagement, but in his judgment, immediate and unilateral withdrawal does not seem the best way to achieve that goal. He has chosen instead the twin course of Vietnamization and negotiation, an honorable moderate course which I believe will serve the interests of both our countries and the interests of peace. This morning the House Republican Conference passed a resolution supporting the President in these efforts. I think these efforts should win the support of almost all of us, Democrats as well as Republicans, in the Congress and in the country at large.

When a quorum of House Members had convened, the postal pay raise bill came up for general debate. My job was to "handle the rule," and then to help lead the opposition to the bill on the floor and to see that the President's position was forcefully represented. I opened with a ten-minute speech in which I said postal workers deserved higher wages, but this raise was ill-timed and inflationary. I answered questions from supporters of the bill, then spent the bulk of the afternoon on the floor following the debate. I had been hoping to appear on a television news show that evening in support of the president's Vietnam policy, but I had to cancel the appearance because the House was still voting on the postal pay raise bill amendments. The bill was finally passed late in the afternoon. The House then moved into a general debate on the Vietnam Moratorium.

At five o'clock I met with a small organization of Congressmen, which we call our "S.O.S." group, in my office. Shortly after six o'clock I went back to the floor of the House, where I engaged in debate with a Democratic critic of the Administration's Vietnam policy. I left at 8:30 to catch a plane for Chicago and a speech the next morning.

Wednesday

This was the first Vietnam Moratorium day. At nine o'clock I spoke to the student body of Elmhurst College in suburban Chicago. After answering a series of pointed questions from the audience, I had to hurry to catch a plane back to Washington to be on the floor for House business in the afternoon. Between taking care of business on the floor, I met with some constituents and a lobbyist, returned telephone calls, and spent a little time working out in the gym of the Rayburn House Office Building next door.

Late that afternoon I flew to Buffalo for a speech at 7:30 before a group of New York State Republican leaders.

Thursday

The morning brought the usual variety of things: legislative and case mail, my schedule of upcoming speeches, plans for an upcoming House Republican Conference breakfast, and an unplanned and somewhat free-wheeling discussion with my aides about campus unrest and the communications gap between political leaders and today's young people.

I had lunch with Rep. Peter Frelinghuysen of New Jersey, and at two, an appointment with a young constituent from Rockford who was looking for a job; at three, my weekly appointment to make a radio tape for stations in my District. Between those matters I went across the street to the House Chamber in the Capitol to vote on the Student Loan bill and the Export Control Act. The House adjourned shortly after six o'clock. I had to cancel a speech scheduled for that evening at Teaneck, New Jersey.

Friday

Another morning of somewhat routine business: I met a constituent at my office at nine o'clock, dictated letters, checked with other Congressmen on the status of legislation, and went over the committee schedule for next week. My legislative assistant briefed me on the Housing and Urban Development bill coming up the following week, and we discussed an amendment I planned to offer, to prohibit restrictions on the use of new building techniques and materials in the construction of low-cost housing.

Late in the morning I left for the airport to fly to Illinois for a speech at Watseka on behalf of a colleague who was unable to keep the appointment. That evening I returned briefly to Rockford for a good night's sleep before flying to Florida the next day for a speech on housing before the Florida Association of Realtors.

Saturday

The speech before the realtors was at 12:30 in Miami. I returned to Washington immediately after my address and was back at my Washington office long enough to sign some mail and catch up on some correspondence.

The schedule I have just outlined is really only a bare skeleton. Many other things come up in the course of an average day that demand time and consideration. For instance, when I am in my office, either talking with an aide or a constituent, or trying to read or write, there is a telephone call about once every five or ten minutes in an average day.

I did not include time out for meals, but often enough there is simply not time to eat a sit-down lunch. Often I just grab a sandwich or go without.

There are the occasional sessions before the television cameras, and much reading about and discussion of legislation, inside and outside of the normal Tuesday morning Rules Committee meetings.

Evenings are often taken by receptions or business meetings of one kind or another. Almost every night I take home a briefcase full of work: legislation pending before the Rules Committee or the House, assorted articles, speech drafts, and other reading matter.

The American Political Science Association estimates that the average Congressman works a sixty-hour week. I should be so lucky! My guess is that for me the figure would be closer to eighty hours, and some weeks considerably more. The demands for speeches are ever-increasing, partly because of the position I hold in the House leadership. At the same time, leadership responsibilities cut in on the time I have for normal legislative and representative functions.

It's a rough, time-consuming, demanding job — but I love it. I wouldn't be here if I didn't. The pressures do often seem unremitting, but the rewards and satisfactions that come from the feeling of total involvement with matters that are important both now and for the future of our country provide the necessary incentives to continue.

5
PRESSURES AND PRINCIPLES IN THE DECISION-MAKING PROCESS

The decision-making process in Congress represents a complex interplay of many different forces; there is no single formula, no single way that a Congressman arrives at a decision on a given issue. Some of the factors that influence a legislator are fairly objective, and some of them, as will be seen, are entirely subjective.

Decision-making often is a matter of weighing various pressures. There are individual pressures from people who express themselves, either in personal visits or in letters, on particular issues, or who have certain wants that they feel ought to be satisfied by the services that a government can provide. Some may even be important political allies or campaign contributors. Then there are group pressures, and these are perhaps the most significant ones: powerful groups in our society, be they labor unions, chambers of commerce, or trade associations, who are interested in a particular piece of legislation. It may be something that benefits them, but it may not be in the general interest. They fail to see that one who would truly represent the people cannot subordinate the overriding public interest to the interests of a particular group.

The communication that I try to maintain with my constituents may at times bring up to several hundred letters a day; normally I try to read them as carefully as time will permit, in an effort to find out what people are thinking at home. Many legislators, including myself, annually send out a poll card seeking constituents' opinions on some of the issues that are expected to be debated in the coming session of Congress. We tabulate these responses in an effort to get some feeling for the public pulse.

Another factor in the decision-making process is what a Congressman reads. I read at least four or five major newspapers a day, in addition to receiving in my office more than twenty newspapers from the 16th District in northwestern Illinois. Though I do not have time to read all of them carefully, they are clipped for me and matters of unusual import or interest are called to my attention. Magazines that I look through when I have a chance range from the *Congressional Quarterly* through *Time, Life,* and *Newsweek,* to *Christianity Today* and *Moody Monthly.* There are many other periodicals and journals, but most of my other reading seems to be confined to reports of Congressional hearings and studies that have been prepared for me by the Library of Congress.

There are a variety of group pressures that make themselves manifest in the legislative process. Here we enter the area of the professional lobbyist. There is something about the term "lobbyist" that carries a bad connotation for many people. Actually, that is quite unfair. There are many trade organizations, many business organizations, labor organizations, and other organizations that exert group pressures, but in a way that I think is entirely compatible with the proper functioning of our political process. They seek to provide information to the thoughtful legislator; they seek to provide opinions that are substantiated by facts that their own organization or other research organizations have developed. So, when we speak of a lobbyist, we are not necessarily talking about a surly, decrepit individual with a cigar in one corner of his mouth, passing a black satchel under the table. Some people make that caricature, and lobbyists of a similar genre unquestionably do exist, but after many years in Washington, I am persuaded that the vast majority of lobbyists are men of good conscience who play a constructive role in our processes of government. This is true as long as you recognize the lobbyist for what he is: a paid protagonist for a particular point of view.

Another factor in the decision-making process is the position of the party. This may be a position formerly taken at a party convention, adopted in the form of a plank as a part of the party platform. Or perhaps the position was adopted in our own more closely knit party structure within the House of Representatives. It may represent a decision taken by our Policy Committee, or by the House Republican Conference, which on occasion will adopt a formal resolution on an important issue. These party positions are not binding in the sense that a member is expelled from the party, or subject to formal discipline, if he chooses to vote what he believes are his own convictions, rather than follow the so-called party line. And yet, obviously, a party position is a very influential factor, especially for a member of the leadership like myself.

Then there is a member's own personal evaluation and study of the hearings and the reports. On an important bill, for example, a House

Committee may sit for weeks. There may be hundreds or even thousands of pages of testimony from witnesses who come from all over the country. Insofar as he can, with the help of his staff, a Congressman sifts through these hearings and studies these reports. This is one of the most valuable means he has of making a personal judgment on a critical issue.

Edmund Burke, the brilliant English Conservative parliamentarian, said that a legislator owes his constituency "not his industry only, but his judgment; and he betrays instead of serving (them) if he sacrifices it to (their) opinion." Some do not agree with that philosophy, but I think most Members of Congress cherish it as a very important part of the representative process. Ultimately a representative, even though he certainly has to regard the opinions of those who have sent him to Washington, must make the final analysis and the final judgment. This is hard for people to accept. It is difficult to say it without seeming a little supercilious, but obviously on some very complicated questions many people read only a single source of information — often biased and slanted — and they form a quick conclusion. Bearing the responsibilities that he does, no Congressman can afford that luxury. He has to consider many different points of view and try to sift out a balanced view of the truth, which is not always an easy job, rather than faithfully follow a particular line.

For me, there's another important factor in my personal decision-making. My Christian convictions also come into play in this process. I want to make it clear that I do not believe there is necessarily a Christian position *per se* on every single social, political, or economic question that comes up. Dedicated Christians can disagree, and disagree widely, on particular political questions. They may all have followed the very same process I have just described in arriving at a thoughtful judgment on a given issue, and yet arrive at different conclusions. Sometimes we tend to believe that Christian conviction is going to lead everyone down the same narrow path to a foreordained truth. It isn't that simple and it doesn't work that way.

But faith can play a vital role in the decision-making process. Often I have occasion to resort to prayer, not in extremity, not as the last resort, but as a wonderful means of giving me peace and assurance that my mind is clear on a particular issue. My own worship experience has often been an important part of the process. On many occasions as I have attended a Sunday morning service (particularly here in Washington where the pastor makes it a regular practice to pray for the President, members

37

of the Supreme Court, and Members of Congress in a very specific and individualized fashion), I have been deeply moved by the thought that he and the congregation were upholding us in prayer. I can also think of sermons that have brought home a spiritual truth with great impact, and have given me a clearer insight into some of the problems that we deal with in the Congress. Personal Bible study is also important to me. There isn't a book that is more influential in my life, or more important in giving me a sense of the Divine purpose that rules all of our lives. This Scripture reading keeps forcefully before me the fact that God does care about what we think and what we do, and how we do it.

The counsel of other Christians can also be helpful. During the debate over the open housing bill in the spring of 1968, talks with some of my Christian friends gave me a great feeling of their depth of concern for this problem, and Christian compassion as revealed in these conversations certainly played a part in the ultimate decision that I made. On other great social questions of our time, whether in talking about trying to alleviate the problem of hunger, or trying to do something to improve housing and slum conditions generally, often talks with fellow Christians have opened my heart because of the concern they have felt.

We have talked about the pressures that are brought to bear on individual legislators in a body like the House of Representatives, and we have discussed the principles that an individual Christian lawmaker in turn tries to bring to bear on the process of decision-making. How are all these pressures and principles reconciled? Is it actually possible to chart a course compatible with personal Christian faith, and to be true to one's convictions despite these pressures?

My answer is short, and I hope not deceptively simple: God can give us, through His grace and power, the wisdom and strength that we lack in and of ourselves. If there is one heart cry that Christians in public office today do make, it is that we would have the wisdom and discernment that is not always there in the human heart, unless it is truly inspired by God Himself.

I pray daily for real wisdom and understanding, to be able to surmount some of these pressures, and to have the courage that is sometimes required to oppose the unremitting demands of one or more of these elements in the complex of individual and group pressures. There are a number of different pressure points on a given issue, but my overriding conviction is that faith and trust in the power of God can aid me in any situation. God is ready to give us real help, real guidance, and more than mere earthly wisdom in coming to the judgments that must be made day in and day out in the halls of Congress. These words from Proverbs have proved their worth to me over and over again: "Trust in the Lord with all thine heart; and lean not unto thine own understanding" (Proverbs 3:5).

I often wish that evangelical Christians would individually and as a group be more effective in presenting their ideas to men in government. Within the institutional church today, it is clearly the liberal wing that speaks most cohesively and dramatically. There are some studies which indicate that evangelicals are preoccupied with salvation to the extent that they believe they are relatively powerless to affect current happenings in our society. We will have more to say about this in a later chapter. It is relevant at this point to record the conviction that men in government can be influenced for good by those who do believe that "Righteousness exalteth a nation: but sin is a reproach to any people" (Proverbs 14:34).

INSTITUTIONS

Every society has its distinctive institutions, which together give form and content to the common life of its people. Over the decade just passed we have seen American institutions called into question at every turn. Some charge that they are outworn and useless; others that they are corrupt and oppressive, and ought to be destroyed. In the next few chapters I would like to take a brief look at some of these institutions, explore the functions they serve in our society, and discuss some of the criticisms that have been leveled against them.

I propose to begin with the Congress, of which I am a member, and then to discuss the Republican Party to which I belong. Many of the criticisms levelled against our institutions have come from young people who will one day be entrusted with the guardianship of those institutions, and so a third chapter is devoted to our alienated youth. The next chapter raises, and tries to answer, the question implicit in so many of youth's criticisms: "Does the System still work?" A final chapter is devoted to the growing malaise of "massification" in our society, and a bold new initiative by President Nixon which may point the way to a reinvigoration of the institutions of American democracy.

6
WHAT KIND OF SOCIETY DO WE WANT?

One of the most significant developments in the 91st Congress has been the beginning of the great "national priorities" debate. Calling for "a reordering of national priorities," many Congressmen and Senators have begun to question whether we need to spend so much and so uncritically on such things as new weapons systems and manned space probes, while pressing human needs go unmet in our decaying cities and depressed rural areas. Republicans and Democrats alike have joined in this public discussion about what kind of society we want to have and how our public resources can be most effectively used to help build and preserve it.

Americans have always subscribed to a highly individualistic social ethic. Partly as a legacy of our Judaeo-Christian heritage, we have traditionally placed a high value on individual human beings and attached great importance to personal freedoms, privacy, and the right of each citizen to live pretty much as he chooses. Much of our lives is indeed governed by individual preference and choice, and many Americans do find fulfillment in pursuing private hopes and personal dreams.

But there is another side to most of our lives, a side shaped by the institutions which comprise our public or common world. In the independent or non-government sector we have our churches, our businesses, our news media, and our Little League teams. In the government sector we have our public schools, our fire departments, armed ser/ices, and anti-poverty agencies. The debate over national priorities has served to focus attention on the quality of these institutions, the values they reflect, and the measures we might take through them to make our society what we would like it to be.

To a large extent our political institutions — and particularly the Congress — provide the arena in which questions like this wi'l be decided. As columnist Jimmy Breslin says, if you are concerned about wh re your society is going, politics is "the only game in town." Our institutions of government are responsible for laying the foundations of our common life. The manner in which we make and administer our laws does have an impact that reaches into virtually every sphere of human activity. We could provide endless examples; perhaps at this point one will suffice. The Tax Reform Act of 1969 did far more than merely affect the collection of federal revenues. In its treatment of charitable contributions, and particularly foundations, it will have a profound effect on how people decide to support many activities in the non-governmental sector of our society.

If and when major changes are necessary to make our institutions more responsive to the needs of the American people, it is Congress that must fashion the laws which will give those changes legitimacy, after careful consideration of the problems to be solved and the possible alternative solutions. Thus in the past decade Congress passed the monumental Civil Rights Act of 1964 and the Voting Rights Act of 1965, both intended to make our society more open and equal to black citizens. We have noted the comprehensive tax reform act of 1969, intended to eliminate the worst inequities of the old system. The need for new means of combating water pollution gave rise to the Water Quality Improvement Act of 1970. Congress is also considering a complete reform of our nation's outdated and self-defeating welfare system. In these and other areas, the Congress, as it does its job, functions to make our institutions of government responsive to changing needs.

The national priorities debate has drawn attention to another aspect of Congressional responsibility, which we call the function of "legislative oversight." Here we see how two of our most important institutions of government, the Presidency and the Congress, cooperate to set the priorities of our federal government. Much of the actual work of Congress in a given year is devoted not to the passage of new laws such as those just cited, but to the oversight and funding of agencies in the Executive Branch. The Departments of Defense, Justice, Health, Education and Welfare, Agriculture, and all the other agencies of the federal government must come to the Congress for a review of their past programs and future needs. The Congress, through the Appropriations Committees of the House and Senate, then provides operating budgets for the coming year or years. This procedure is intended to provide a check on the activities of the Executive Departments, which otherwise might feel responsible only to a strong-willed President or to their own inner bureaucracies.

If we assume that the amount of money and resources a society devotes to certain activities is at least a rough index of how important it feels those activities are, relative to others which might also have a claim on its scarce funds, then we can see how the appropriations process in the Congress gives concrete expression to the debate over national priorities. At the beginning of each calendar year the President submits his budget proposals for the fiscal year, beginning the next July. Congress then allocates the monies in the federal purse and pays the actual bills, in the process deciding, for example, whether we are spending too much to subsidize education and not enough to fight crime. Thus the appropriations voted by Congress in a given year, seen as percentages of the total federal budget, provide a rough outline of our national priorities (though not by any means an exact one, for many activities which we value highly, such as education and law enforcement, are funded largely by state and local governments).

The heaviest motif of the budget submitted to the Congress by President Nixon in February, 1970, was the need to cut government spending in a major effort to check inflation. The effort to cut waste and extravagance from federal expenditures has claimed perhaps more of my time and energies than any other single issue during my years in Congress. But in 1969 and 1970 there was cause for even more concern than usual, for five years of rising federal outlays under President Lyndon Johnson had fueled a rise in prices and costs that was threatening to pauperize even middle-income Americans, let alone the poor and the senior citizens whose incomes are relatively fixed. Thus the Nixon budget for fiscal 1971 — the year running from July 1, 1970, to June 30, 1971 — emphasized a tight upper limit on spending and a modest surplus of unexpended tax receipts, to take some of the heat out of the national economy and check the price-cost spiral.

But there were other important themes in the new Nixon budget. Of particular interest was the relative comparison, in fiscal 1970 and fiscal 1971, between military spending and what Congressmen and Senators like to call "human resources." We will have more to say shortly about this aspect of the 1971 budget.

By far the largest share of the 1970 federal tax dollar — some forty-one percent — had gone to current military spending, under a budget whose major outlines had been shaped by President Johnson before he left office in January, 1969. Another large percentage — probably more than fifteen percent — went to defense-related fixed costs such as interest on the public debt incurred in past wars, veteran's benefits, and military pay raises.

In *The Economy of Death*, Richard J. Barnet makes the claim that the United States spends more than seventy cents out of each tax dollar on past, present, and future wars. Our studies indicate that Barnet has overstated the case considerably, but I do not think we have to accept his statistics to understand his point. Whether we have been spending fifty-five percent or seventy percent of our federal taxes on armies and armaments, the cold statistics tell us that our country has been devoting a large, perhaps disproportionate share of its resources to war and preparation for war. The question implicit in recent budgets was whether we really care more about our ability to fight foreign wars than we do about the quality of our life here at home.

The trend toward increased military budgets had been rising sharply in the past few years. Between 1948 and 1970 our military spending increased some 680 percent, from 11.8 billion dollars to 80 billion. From 1961 to 1968 it rose 70 percent. On Vietnam alone we have been spending from 25 to 30 billion dollars a year. Increases of this order did not just happen. Someone, at some point along the way, honestly saw a need for them. Our rising defense budgets were based on assumptions about the nature and size of the foreign military threat facing the United States, some of which had been accepted pretty much without question since the early post-World War Two period. What we have had to ask ourselves is whether the military threat facing us today is the same as it was then. If it is different, how does it differ and what adjustments should we therefore make in our national defense posture?

As an example, for a long time American strategic planning had been based on the "two plus one doctrine" — the notion that to guarantee our national security we should be prepared at all times to fight simultaneously a major war in Europe, a major war in Asia, and a minor war in our own hemisphere. But how likely was it that we would ever be called upon to fight two and a half major wars at once? And how likely was it that we would be willing, even if able, to do it — especially in light of our experience in Vietnam? Reduced commitments and rising costs rendered the "two plus one doctrine" obsolete, and in the fall of 1969 Defense Secretary Melvin Laird announced that henceforth American strategic planning would be based on a capacity to fight one major war and one minor one at the same time, if this should ever prove necessary. This kind of realism should allow substantial savings in our burgeoning military budget.

Much of the Congressional criticism of military spending habits has been due to growing evidence of sheer waste. Ever since I can remember, the federal government has been notorious for waste. But it is only in recent months that many of us in the Congress have begun to realize that the Defense Department is no more immune to wasteful practices and procedures than the Department of Agriculture, or Health, Education and Welfare, or Labor.

Let me give two examples. For fiscal year 1970, we in the Congress authorized 275 million dollars to procure a new carrier-based fighter plane called the F-14, in addition to 175 million dollars for research and development costs. No one during the debate that took place on this issue was able to depict a scenario in which that plane would be useful. We don't really think that in an all-out nuclear war — and the only enemy that we foresee in that regard would be either the Soviet Union or Red China — we would be in a position to use this particular plane or weapons system to advantage. Yet, almost automatically, we accepted the idea that we needed it.

We have also talked for some time about the necessity for a follow-on bomber to the B-52. The Air Force has now developed the AMSA, or Advanced Manned Strategic Aircraft. In the 1970 budget 100 million dollars was allocated for research and development of this bomber. Yet very little thought had been given to whether or not we needed a new generation of heavy bombers. We rely for our strategic offense against the Soviet Union — and as far as that goes, for our defense, too — on our nuclear power, our strategic missiles, our ICBM's, and our Polaris submarine fleet with its 656 nuclear-tipped missiles.

Some of us in the Congress felt that this was a question that deserved a little more thought. Perhaps in 1970 the threat that faces us is not precisely the same threat that faced us when this program was conceived. Also, there is the enormous cost to consider, particularly in view of the long lead times that are required to produce these extremely sophisticated weapons systems — eight or nine years in the case of AMSA. It is estimated that this one program alone will cost 23 billion dollars by the time it is fully implemented. After the bombers are ready and we have spent the entire 23 billion, we may wake up and wonder whether or not this is the kind of weapon that we need to defend ourselves in 1978. Some now believe it is, but other military experts feel it is wholly superfluous, and that it would merely add to the overkill power we already possess, at great and unnecessary cost to the American taxpayer.

Thus during the first session of the 91st Congress a growing number of Congressmen, myself included, came to feel that we could spend a lot less on defense and a lot more on urgent domestic needs without in any way compromising our national security. We were faced with the problem of limited resources to handle a great number of costly propositions. Unfortunately, we could not do what Jesus did with the loaf of bread to feed the multitudes. We had one loaf and that had to be cut in such a way as to derive maximum benefit for a maximum number of people. This meant a reallocation of resources. The first place to look was that sector which was getting the lion's share of the loaf, the current military budget.

At the same time that the national priorities debate was opening in the Congress, President Nixon and his Budget Director, Robert Mayo, were beginning their own assessment of how federal resources could be more effectively allocated to meet our most pressing domestic needs. Defense Secretary Melvin Laird was especially helpful in identifying areas of military spending which could be cut back without compromising our national security.

The table on page 52 illustrates the dramatic turn-around in federal spending proposed by the president in his budget for fiscal 1971. Military spending has been cut by almost six billion dollars in absolute terms, and its share of the total federal budget has declined from forty to thirty-seven percent. On the other hand, proposed spending for "human resources" — health, education and welfare, social security, and veterans' benefits — has been increased from thirty-seven to forty-one percent. In one year we have the possibility of significantly reordering our priorities if the president's major proposals are approved by the Congress, as I hope and expect.

I believe President Nixon has shown real leadership in working to turn our national priorities around. He deserves our support. If I thought for a moment that our national security really demanded a full forty percent of the federal budget, then I would be the first to insist that we look elsewhere for needed resources. But having studied the problem for months, I am convinced that we can save billions just by eliminating some of the waste and inefficiency now prevalent in defense spending. We can save even more by reexamining the underlying strategic assumptions that have forced us to build such a variety of weapons systems and maintain such a large number of troops around the world.

These resources can be used to reorder our priorities in a hundred ways. They can be used to attack the roots of decay in our cities and to make our rural environments liveable and attractive once more. It has been estimated that over the next decade alone we could spend a trillion dollars — a sum too vast for anyone to comprehend — just to rebuild the inner cities of America, to relieve and remove the scabrous slums which have bred conditions that have festered into violence in recent years. In the field of education, it has been said that we could, for the cost of just one squadron of supersonic bombers, operate for a generation a great university that would minister to the educational needs of young people.

I have argued that it will do us little good to be armed to the teeth to deter external threats, if we are not able to cope with the internal threats posed by pressing domestic problems. When we talk about the security of the United States, we must consider internal as well as external conditions. And the internal conditions today are such that they do pose a real threat to the continued security of our country.

Anyone who has walked our slums and seen the pathetic sight of children living and growing up in the stench of that kind of environment will understand that we may be breeding a generation of young Americans who are not going to be equipped and prepared to give our country the inner strength it must have to compete against the forces that would destroy us if they could. Anyone who has had the fetid smell of a rotting slum in his nostrils, or picked his way through one of the human slag heaps that are to be found in big cities across our country, will understand that people living and dying in conditions like this soon lose both the hope and the desire to make a meaningful contribution to their society, which instead they grow to hate.

We will have more to say in later chapters about the conditions that pass for living and learning environments in our urban and rural slums. Suffice it to say here that we will not be able to make a real start in relieving these conditions until we have completed the task of reordering our priorities.

Among our first priorities must be a commitment to make this country a better place in which to live for all Americans. As Housing and Urban Development Secretary George Romney put it:

The greater struggle to which we should now address ourselves (is) the rebuilding of our cities; the cleansing and improvement of our environment; the elimination of racial prejudice and social tensions; the realization of the equal justice, equal opportunity and equal human dignity which are the birthright of all Americans.

In that speech, delivered significantly enough on the day of the first moon landing, Secretary Romney had the courage to suggest that we content ourselves with achieving these goals rather than with setting another priority goal in space. In his words:

How much greater would be our contribution to the well-being of all Americans if we were to make massive new investments to improve the lot of man on earth — rather than to divert those resources to land an American on still another planet.

Twenty years ago Congress set the goal of a "decent home and suitable living environment for every American family." We are now faced with the severest housing and environmental crises in our history. By way of contrast, nine years ago we said we would put a man on the moon; and in July, 1969, we did just that, after a massive commitment of resources, manpower, and technology. I am proud of that achievement, but I also think the time has come to apply that same kind of effort to meeting our twenty-year-old pledge here on earth. To build a decent, just, humane society in America will require the commitment of vast resources under the direction of our most talented leaders.

But money alone will not suffice, and we err if we think we can transform our society overnight by changing a few figures in the national balance sheet. Beyond the priorities of better housing, better jobs, better education, and better health care, the first priority that I would like to see established for our society is a recognition of the absolute importance of spiritual as opposed to purely material values. Slavery existed in this country until we conceded that it was an abasement of the spirit of man to consider him as a mere chattel. We will continue to countenance an abridgment of human freedoms through various forms of discrimination until we are willing to assert this respect for human personality despite the material costs that may be involved. There is an important corollary. It is simply that love rather than wealth, power, or human knowledge must rule in human affairs if we are truly to carry out God's perfect will. For those who dismiss such a notion as completely visionary and impractical, given the kind of world in which we live, there is a short and simple answer: It has never been tried.

Some time ago the distinguished Dean of Harvard College gave up his prestigious position to accept the presidency of a small and impoverished Negro college in Alabama, not for power or prestige, and certainly not because it offered greater material advantages, but because of his love and concern for his fellow-man. Our problem today, whether it involves improving education or solving any one of a myriad problems, is that we lack enough dedicated and committed men and women.

The great philosopher Alfred North Whitehead once said, "The major advances in civilization are processes which all but wreck the society in which they occur." As we view the disorder of our age and reflect on the trauma of the decade past, it is often difficult to believe that we have actually made any progress toward building a better society. The pessimist says that the rate of our social metabolism has accelerated too rapidly and that the resulting changes in our body politic are proof of an unhealthy society. The optimist cheerily predicts that we are on the threshold of a great new era in which man can finally free himself from the enslaving forces of his environment and reach his full spiritual dimension.

As a self-professed moderate, I believe that we are somewhere in between. At times, in our desire to cast off ancient shibboleths, we have not been careful enough to preserve fundamental values. In other matters we have clung too tenaciously to archaic ways, which in the poet's words "have become uncouth, because truth must ever upward and onward be." We are in that phase of human existence that inspired the title for this book, a paraphrase of the words of Matthew Arnold: "between two worlds, one dead, the other struggling to be born."

We cannot resurrect the halcyon days that characterized a world still largely pastoral in its pursuits. Technology cannot be repealed. There is no King Lud to decree that all the machines should be destroyed. We cannot turn back the pages of our history, in hopes of finding a better society in the past than we have in the present. No, the pages of history turn inexorably toward the future, and it is in that direction we must look if we would truly build a better world. Let future pages record that we did not shirk that challenge and that responsibility.

As a Christian, I do not believe that of our own power we can ever build that perfect society which we all seek. We have tried and failed too many times, bringing pain on ourselves and suffering on others. But neither would I agree with those who say that the prospect of improving our world is bleaker today than it has ever been before, that we are more impotent to do good than at any time in man's history. For the Scriptures teach us that man's extremity is God's opportunity. As Paul puts it in his letter to the Church at Corinth:

> Yet we believe now that we had this experience of coming to the end of our tether that we might learn to trust, not in ourselves, but in God who can raise the dead. It was God who preserved us from imminent death, and it is he who still preserves us (II Corinthians 1:9-10, J. B. Phillips translation).

REORDERING OUR PRIORITIES: THE CHANGING FEDERAL BUDGET

Spending by Function	Millions of Dollars (Estimates)			% of Total Budget	
	1970	1971	Difference	1970	1971
National Defense	79,432	73,583	− 5,849	40	37
Social Security & Welfare	43,832	50,384	+ 6,552	22	26
Interest on Public Debt	17,821	17,799	− 22	9	9
Health	13,265	14,957	+ 1,692	7	8
Commerce & Transportation	9,436	8,785	− 651	5	4
Veterans' Benefits	8,681	8,475	− 206	4	4
Education & Manpower Training	7,538	8,129	+ 591	4	4
Agriculture & Rural Development	6,343	5,364	− 979	3	3
International Affairs & Finance	4,113	3,589	− 524	2	2
Space	3,886	3,400	− 486	2	2
Housing & Urban Development	3,046	3,781	+ 735	2	2
Natural Resources	2,485	2,503	+ 18	1	1
Allowances for:					
General Administration	3,620	4,084	464	2	2
Revenue Sharing with States		275	275		
Civilian & Military Pay Increases	175	1,400	1,225		
Contingencies	300	900	600		
Undistributed Intragovernmental Transactions	− 6,088	− 6,639		(3)	(4)
TOTAL SPENDING	197,885	200,771	2,886	100	100

Source: New York Times, Feb. 3, 1970

7
A
REPUBLICAN
CREDO

For more than a hundred years American political life has been dominated by two great institutions, the Republican and Democratic Parties. Issues change, coalitions shift, personalities come and go. Still the elephant and the donkey remain; they are among the most durable symbols of the distinctive political process known as American Democracy.

I suspect that many of us naturally think of ourselves as either Republicans or Democrats, but without really giving much thought as to *why*. Often we simply follow family tradition or local custom. We Americans are a pragmatic people. We understand political parties in their role as vehicles for putting politicians in office, but do not pay as much attention to the important function they serve in expressing basic philosophical differences about principles of government. The tradition of political *power* is strong in America, but the tradition of political *philosophy* has not taken root as deeply on this side of the Atlantic as it has in, say, England.

I am a Republican, not only by tradition but by conviction as well. I believe the principles for which the Republican Party stands are solid and sure, and that they have served our country well. In the next few pages I would like to set down those principles as I view them in their historical context, and then show why I believe they are as valid today as when they were first formed. It is sometimes said, half seriously and half in jest, that every politician finds occasions when he must rise above principle. However, I believe that only the most cynical observer would deny the continuing validity of certain basic political beliefs.

The Republican Party was born on a cold day in March, 1854, in a little town called Ripon, Wisconsin. The fifty-three men who gathered there were of all major political persuasions — Freesoilers, Whigs, and Democrats. As moderates they rejected the extremism of both the Abolitionists and the Know-Nothings, but they were united in opposition to the extension of slavery into Kansas, a free territory. To these men, slavery was a moral, social, and political scourge. The party they founded rode this issue to victory in the presidential election of 1860, six years after the meeting in Ripon. The Republican candidate, Abraham Lincoln, put the matter squarely and forcefully:

> This declared indifference to the spread of slavery I cannot but hate. I hate it because of the monstrous injustice of slavery itself. I hate it because it deprives our republican example of its just influence in the world; enables the enemies of free institutions with plausibility to taunt us as hypocrites; causes the real friends of freedom to doubt our sincerity; and especially because it forces so many good men among ourselves into an open war against the very fundamental principles of civil liberties . . . .

Thus the first principle of historic Republicanism is the extension of freedom, based on a deep regard for human *rights*.

Within a few short years after the founding of the party, the nation was rent by civil war, and President Lincoln had articulated a second great tenet of Republican faith — preservation of the Union. Though few realize it today, this principle became so important that in the campaign of 1864 Republicans actually changed their name to become known as the Union Party. Again we hear the great Lincoln, his message now one of *reconciliation:*

> . . . . With malice toward none, with charity for all, with firmness in the right as God gives us to see the right, let us strive on to finish the work we are in, to bind up the nation's wounds . . . .

So a second historic tenet of Republicanism is the preservation of national unity, the appeal for national reconciliation. To become a party of sectional or special interest would be to betray the vision of our founders.

Still another principle of our political creed emerged during the years of Republican ascendancy at the close of the nineteenth and the beginning of the twentieth century. It was the principle of fiscal restraint, or *responsibility* in government. Conscious of the need to preserve order and economy in the social and political affairs of the nation, Republicans showed no appetite for the prescriptions of those who advocated various tenuous theories about tinkering with the supply of money and credit. The nation rejected the populism of William Jennings Bryan with its promise of cheap money. Republicans insisted on the balanced budget and the sound dollar. Some claimed that the Grand Old Party had sold out to Wall Street, but during a long stretch of history between the

Civil War and up to almost the time of World War One, the great majority of voters repeatedly demonstrated that they felt the country was in good hands.

Finally, in reaction against the excesses of the tumultuous New Deal, a fourth Republican article of faith took shape: decentralization of power. Where the Democrats put their faith in big government and powerful agencies centralized in Washington, Republicans held to the belief that most human social problems could be most effectively solved by the people themselves, working under local leadership with direct responsibility. The centralization of power in Washington during the New Deal upset the system of checks and balances— not just as between the three branches of government, but as between the levels of local, state and federal government, and between the government and the people themselves — upon which our federal government is based. In espousing efforts to reassert this balance between our institutions, the Republican Party enters the decade of the 1970's as a party of *reform*.

Among the most important principles of historic and contemporary Republicanism, then, are rights, reconciliation, responsibility, and reform.

Are those principles still sound? Will they serve us, as a party and as a nation, in the uncertain, perhaps perilous decade of the 1970's? I think the answer is an emphatic *yes*.

Surely there can be no question about the need for rededication to the first principle of Republicanism — the extension of freedom. The old enemy, slavery, is gone. But in its place stalk ignorance, poverty, disease, prejudice, and discrimination, the threat of environmental extinction, of moral depravity encouraged by a society which has lost much of its earlier idealism. All these are foes which seek to lay waste the substance of true freedom.

I do not suggest that as a political party we have the final solution to all of these problems. If freedom depends on a pluralistic society, and I believe it does, then we must look to church and home and school as well — and not least to the individual himself. But as a political party, and especially as the Republican Party, we should be providing leadership in the continuing effort to extend freedom of opportunity and basic human rights to each and every one of our citizens. The position of the Republican Party on voting rights seems to me critical in this regard. It was this belief that led me to oppose a dilution of the strong 1965 Voting Rights Act, for it seemed to me that such a course of action would be to abdicate the historic leadership of the Republican

Party in the battle to extend the limits of freedom. We continue to need a Republican emphasis on basic human *rights*.

Perhaps it would be well to observe at this point that on the issue of the extension of the Voting Rights Act of 1965, I broke with a majority of my party in the House of Representatives, and with the Attorney General and others in the Administration who had recommended what I regarded as a weaker version of the 1965 law. There are those occasions obviously when, even though members of a political party share a common fealty to a basic principle, they part company over the manner in which that political principle should be implemented in specific legislation.

Another principle of historic Republicanism, the preservation of the Union, found an echo in the 1968 campaign theme of President Nixon: "Bring us together." Never in recent years has our society been so rent in so many ways as it was during the turbulent decade of the Sixties. As a nation, we are torn between white and black, between an entrenched older generation and anti-establishment youth, between the affluent and the poor. I believe that President Nixon is sincerely trying to bridge these gaps, but he needs the support of the entire nation. The Republican Party must continue to be a party of *reconciliation*.

The President has demonstrated his belief in the Republican doctrine of fiscal restraint. Indeed he inherited a fiscal situation which fairly cried out for the application of this principle. Richard Nixon, seeking restraint and responsibility in government, was quick to realize that the impact of another round of deficit spending on the economy would be disastrous. He has recommended relatively few new programs of a costly variety; instead he has dedicated his Administration to a careful, balanced reappraisal of the limits of government power. Instead of promises, there have been some select but significant proposals, carefully studied, for improving the present operations and programs of the federal government without bursting the budgetary constraints that must be observed if the battle against inflation is to be won.

I should say at this point that this battle is only beginning, and I would hope that Republicans in Congress can rally behind the president and behind this fundamental tenet of Republicanism, fiscal restraint. This is not to say that money will not be required to solve the mounting social and environmental problems that beset us as we enter a new decade. No, it is only to say that our approach to those problems must be realistic as well as imaginative, conscious of costs and the impact on an overheated national economy, responsible as well as bold. Here the Republican Party has made and can continue to make a distinctive contribution to American political life. The G.O.P. must continue to speak for *responsibility* in government.

Again when we look at the fourth tenet of traditional Republican faith, decentralization of power, we find that President Nixon has taken the leadership as no Republican spokesman has done in a generation. In the "New Federalism" he has begun one of the most imaginative attempts in this century to turn the massive, musclebound federal bureaucracy around. In his proposals for welfare reform, manpower retraining, and the sharing of federal revenues with the states, the President has put forward a program for actually reversing the flow of power, money, and responsibility to Washington.

I do not believe the implications of this approach have yet been fully appreciated. In an era when many Americans are beginning to lose confidence in some of the central institutions of our society, when we appear to have lost control over the course of technology, economic development, urban sprawl and decay, and environmental pollution — here is a program that will put responsibility for problem-solving, and the resources to do it, back in the hands of the people. This is participatory democracy at its imaginative best. In President Nixon's words, "The essence of freedom is that each of us shares in the shaping of his own destiny."

The point of all this is that, in implementing the Republican principle of decentralization of power, President Nixon has once again made the Republican Party a party of *reform*. I want the Republican Party to be clearly identified in the public mind as a driving force behind the reformation of our political and social structures. There are, to be quite candid, some within the ranks of our party who are so comfortable in the old ways that new initiatives in such areas as welfare and manpower retraining stimulate scant enthusiasm. They perceive little, if any, need to reorder our national priorities and to pursue such goals as arms control and population control. With them, Republicanism is like the old time religion — "What's good enough for grandpa is good enough for me." But we are beginning to hear new young voices in the Party, and I think that with their help we can muster the support the President needs to make the Republican Party a party of reform.

But lest we become complacent, it may be well to point out now that there are shoals ahead, dangers which could threaten our unity and effectiveness as a political party capable of governing the United States of America. One such danger is sectionalism.

Much has been written about the so-called "Southern Strategy." Is it real? If so, what is it? And what would it mean for the future growth of the Republican Party? There may be a short-sighted few who see an Emerging Republican Majority based on writing off one or more sections or groups within our country. The charge has been made that the Nixon Administration is making a calculated attempt to woo the conservative South at the expense of the more liberal Northeast. I feel that the president himself has clearly repudiated a "Southern Strategy," or any other strategy based on sectional interests. I believe he understands that such a strategy would be folly for the party and tragedy for the nation.

It is perhaps worth mentioning that this controversy is hardly new. It goes back long before the Civil War, to the founding of the Republic. James Madison, in the Federalist Paper No. 10, said that among the advantages of a well-constructed union, none deserves more emphasis than its tendency to brake and control the violence of faction that has torn and divided us and disturbed the peace and tranquility of our land. It is only as we can unite these factions that we will have surcease from the domestic strife that so dominated the sixties.

But if the Republican Party cannot afford a "Southern Strategy," does that mean that we write off a strategy for the South? No. For a hundred years, the South has had a one-party system of government. Now, a vigorous Republican Party, led by young and attractive candidates, is emerging in the South to challenge moribund Democrats for the leadership of this great region.

As a party we need a strategy for the South. In shaping that strategy, we must reject the pull of sectional interest and prejudice. Our party must be inclusive, not exclusive. As our society is complex and varied, so must we preserve the party's responsibility to speak to all those needs and concerns. Our challenge is to make the Republican Party safe for diversity.

There is another shoal which we must avoid, and that is the danger of polarization in our body politic. Some political commentators have become accustomed to calling the Democratic Party the party of the young, the poor, and the blacks. At the present time, much of the appeal of the national Democratic Party is aimed at the "out" groups in our society — the poor and the black, the "alienated educated," and the young.

But Republicans cannot afford to leave these groups entirely to the Democrats. We cannot afford to become the party of the elderly, the affluent, and the white. For the young will elect tomorrow's presidents. The educated will lead in the battle against tomorrow's challenges. And the poor and the black will dream tomorrow's dreams.

No, we need and we want a Party that speaks to all the American people, not just a few. The challenge may become even more difficult as our nation threatens to become even more divided, but we have the internal resources and the will to provide the leadership our country needs.

Our Party has leaders who will face the challenge of the 1970's with integrity, responsibility, imagination, and renewed faith in American institutions and ideals. Only this kind of leadership will call forth the best that is in us. Nothing more is needed. Nothing less will do.

But leadership is not all we need. Participation is vital to the process of American democracy, and I can think of no better way to close this chapter than with a few words about the value of participation in the party system. Although America has been called a nation of joiners, the fact remains that most Americans do not belong to any organization that represents them in the political system. In other words, they are without any organizational affiliations in government. Only one American in twenty-five reports membership in an explicitly political club or organization which he considers to be involved in any way in political or governmental affairs.

My guess is the percentage would be even smaller for Christians. I do not believe the political clubhouse should become a substitute for the house of worship. What I am suggesting is that the evangelical should remove the blinders of indifference and use his peripheral vision to see the need for Christian influence in solving our social and political problems.

I would further suggest that a major goal of every Christian ought to be participation in some truly meaningful way in the political process. One of my favorite stories concerning the great evangelist Dwight L. Moody comes immediately to mind. He was seen hurrying down North Clark Street in Chicago by one of his parishioners who politely inquired of Mr. Moody where he was going.

"Why, I'm going to my precinct polling place to vote," he replied.

"Mr. Moody, I thought you always told us we were citizens of heaven. Why are you so concerned about an election here on earth?"

To this the evangelist replied with some asperity, "Yes, I'm a citizen of the heavenly commonwealth, but right now I'm paying my taxes here in Cook County, Illinois."

Bad government, corrupt politicians, and the looting of the public treasury occur because of citizen neglect. If we as Christians don't care enough to see that good men are put into office, and if as a result there is a breakdown in honest and efficient public administration, we must share the responsibility. Rousseau, the eighteenth century philosopher, was even more pointed with his reminder that "as soon as any man says of the affairs of State — 'what does it matter to me' — then the State may be given up for lost."

As the title of this book indicates, it was not written as a polemic designed to win adherents for the Republican Party. I dare to hope that it may serve to arouse the latent interest of some Christians who have had little interest in actively participating in the affairs of a political party or organization. I would leave to each of you the decision as to which party best represents your idea of the course our nation should follow. As an active Republican, I have tried to explain my own personal choice of a political vehicle and my own hopes and dreams as to the principles it will follow. Like all human institutions, a political party is at best an imperfect instrument to carry out the lofty purposes to which it professes allegiance. However, a political party has its contemporary role and mission defined by those activists who join its ranks. It is they who use the party machinery to elect themselves and candidates of their persuasion to positions of authority, both within the party itself and to public office. Christians, who are bidden to be the salt of the earth, have an inescapable responsibility to assert their influence in this area of human affairs.

8
OUR
ALIENATED
YOUTH:
STRANGE AND
ESTRANGED

The current crop of red-blooded American boys and girls has undoubtedly unleashed more grief, concern, shock, fear, amazement, hope, and confusion among their elders than any previous generation their elders can remember. Who are these people, offspring of our loins and scions of our own homes?

Arlo Guthrie, the unlikely hero of that improbable film *Alice's Restaurant*, says of them in an interview with the *New York Times* (January 11, 1970):

> We're not a whole group of people involved in a plot. Some look strange. They act strange. Some look ferocious. Some look gentle. They do things that are paradoxical, that make no sense at all. It's only by making no sense that you can make some sense, by having no self-gratifying goal that you can ever really fulfill yourself. Until everybody finds that out, they're going to be uptight, upset, popping uppers, downers, drinking booze, smoking dope. Instant glory!

Arlo sounds vaguely reassuring, despite the luxuriant foliage that distresses those of us who were taught that barbers must earn a living too. But what of the thirteen-year-old boy who says, in a collection of essays published by Random House and entitled *Growing Up Radical*, "The United States enslaves, oppresses, silences, and murders. If we dare to question, or worse, to protest, our leaders are squashed . . . ." Coming from a thirteen-year-old, that doesn't sound quite so innocent.

On 15 October 1969, the first Vietnam Moratorium Day, I spoke to the student body of Elmhurst College in suburban Chicago. Just before I began my speech, the local leader of the Students for a Democratic Society grabbed the microphone. Proceeding to denounce me and anyone with my views, he proposed a total boycott of the meeting, then marched dramatically down the center aisle and led his followers from the hall.

The great majority of students stayed and listened to what I had to say, though it was evident from their questions that many were genuinely troubled by my support of President Nixon's moderate policy of phased withdrawal from Vietnam. What impressed me, however, was that the young man who denounced my views did so without even knowing what they were. If I needed any proof of the generation gap, I found it that day at Elmhurst College.

Shortly thereafter I had the experience of attending a concert by Arlo Guthrie himself on the campus of Georgetown University in Washington. I went partly to ease the strain of a *Kultur Kampf* then raging in our household between myself and my sixteen-year-old daughter, Eleanora. Having made some disparaging remarks about the amplified sounds that were threatening to cause large ceiling cracks in the various rooms of our house, and my preference for Brahms over the Beatles, I grudgingly consented to attend Mr. Guthrie's performance to obtain a more balanced perspective. Although I went and I heard, I was not conquered. But at least I learned that the ringing in my ears was not simply the result of high blood pressure.

All this is by way of underlining the point that young people and older people in our society today seem to be having more difficulty understanding and communicating with each other than at any time since I can remember. The size of the generation gap troubles me, for if a chasm too great to span suddenly yawns between young and old, then it seems clear that much that we value in American society will eventually be lost.

I believe it would be tragic if we as adults lose all capacity to listen to youth, to learn their language, and to translate into that language the values we have learned to cherish. Similarly, it would be tragic if young people become so strident in their criticism of established institutions and the older generation that they turn off even those who sympathize with their desire for change, or if they become so alienated that they no longer care to listen to what their more thoughtful elders have to say.

Why this gap between the generations? The reasons for it are many and complicated, but we can identify several of the major trends that have contributed to the growing sense of distance between youth and age in our society.

First and foremost, there has been a fantastic increase in the rate of change in our culture generally. Journalist Lola Smith says we have made change an American religion, and one of the tenets of the new faith is that life and growth end somewhere about age thirty. Young people tend to be more receptive to change than older people, and if it is true that change is coming to play a more and more important role in our society and culture, then older people must be willing to overcome much of their natural resistance to this inevitable phenomenon. At the same time, as Mrs. Smith points out, we cannot afford to become a society which hates its adults. For then what happens when neurotically anti-adult youth become adults themselves? In itself, change is neither good nor bad. It can be a necessary means of achieving desired ends, but it should not, I believe, be made into an article of blindly accepted faith.

Another important reason for the generation gap is what young people candidly call the hypocrisy of the older generation. We preach equality, opportunity, and justice for all. Yet it is plain to today's youth that we have failed to honor our own pledge to many of our own people. We urge young people to think for themselves, then get upset when they become critical of our own cherished institutions. We preach peace, yet spend a substantial portion of our gross national product making, preparing, and paying for war. We hold property rights to be inviolate, yet feel no compunction about despoiling and plundering the public property of our lakes, rivers, air, forests, and parks. It is perhaps small wonder that many idealistic young people become disillusioned when they see how many of our ideals are somewhat tarnished around the edges.

A third important factor in the alienation of the young is what has been called the anesthesia of affluence. I can remember how hard my parents worked during the lean years of the 1930's just to provide a decent living for our family. Those of us who grew up during that time understandably put great store on economic and financial security. But today's middle class youth have never known deprivation, and perhaps it is understandable why they look beyond the measures of security and success that were so meaningful to an older generation and throw themselves into an often agonizing, sometimes destructive search for deeper meaning.

Another factor is the decline of adult authority. The pressures of modern life have taken a heavy toll in family ties, and parents and children often do not spend the time together that they once did. I can recall that when I was a boy the evening meal was a time of family fellowship; among other things, father would bring out the Bible, read a chapter, and lead the family in prayer. How different it is today, with everyone rushing hither and yon to various activities, classes, clubs, and what not.

Along with adult authority, the authority of the church has been in decline. In part at least, I believe we have to fault the church itself for not communicating the eternal truths of God's Word in a language that young people can understand. Too often the well-springs of imagination have been dry, and we have relied on the dead clichés of an earlier generation to communicate the living truth of the good news. Young people today are searching desperately for deeper meaning, and as Christians we fail our Lord instead of serving Him if we do not get their message and give them His.

The decline of authority has been accompanied by another curious phenomenon, which I think it is important for adults to try to understand. If you talk to young people today, you find that the heroes of an earlier generation have disappeared. In their place are poems and posters celebrating a far different kind of hero: the down and out, the poor, the black, the revolutionary, the strange. It is as if young people were trying to say to the adult world: "We have gone as far as we want to along the road traveled by successful, beautiful, powerful, sophisticated people. We found nothing on that road that met the needs we feel, and we are trying a different road for a while."

It was in the 1960's that the young began their sustained assault on the bastions of American society. During this period there were two great movements — the civil rights movement and the Vietnam peace movement — which more than any others shaped the attitudes and values of this strange and estranged generation. The ranks of the civil rights movement were drawn almost exclusively from the young, from Southern black students and Northern white students who joined hands to try to break the hold of prejudice and discrimination that had denied to so many black Americans the freedom to enter the mainstream of American life.

The successes and failures of the civil rights movement had important psychological effects on the young Americans who became involved in it. Progress often seemed slow, and many injustices persisted, making some believe that change would never come in time to salvage their own hopes for America. On the other hand, many could see real gains, however painfully won, and it restored their faith in the possibility of making this country the kind of free and open society that their textbooks had said it was. On the whole, this movement caught and channeled effectively the tremendous reformist zeal of many of our most idealistic young people.

The Vietnam peace movement began in the middle years of the Sixties, as our country became more and more embroiled in a land war in that small Southeast Asian country. There was confusion at first about whether the war was basically caused by Communist aggression, colonial exploitation, insurgent nationalism, or civil conflict. But it was increasingly evident, to many of the young especially, that American arms were for some reason meeting with little success; that much blood and treasure was being spilled; and that many Vietnamese, even anti-communists, resented our presence there. To these young people it was unclear whether we were supporting a democracy or a dictatorship, and in any case it looked to them as if we might have to destroy Vietnam in order to save it. They began to feel that at best we had no business being in Vietnam, and at worst we had intervened on the wrong side.

Thus the protests began, then escalated; draft cards were burned; the resistance began; many draft-age young men chose to go to jail or renounce their citizenship rather than fight in what they considered an immoral and unconstitutional war. The bitterness and intransigence that we see in so many of our young people today reflects, I believe, the fact that, unlike the civil rights movement, the Vietnam peace movement showed no early successes. Even after the dazzling display of youth power in the McCarthy campaign for the presidency, what successes there were proved hard to measure, and at times seemed illusory as the war dragged on and on, taking lives as casually and anonymously as a steam roller lays down asphalt. The lesson seemed to be that no matter how hard young people tried, nothing they did could slow the juggernaut of war. Perhaps the inevitable outcome was that some, in their frustration, would give up all hope of having an impact by peaceful means and would turn to making bombs.

It seems to me that a high tide of youthful idealism and commitment was reached in the McCarthy campaign of 1968. The real tragedy of Chicago was not the violence done to bodies in the streets but the violence done to hopes in the minds of young people — and I speak now not as a Republican or a Democrat but as an American who cherishes the value of participation in American politics. The lesson of Chicago seemed to be: Don't get involved, for the system will beat you in the end. The post-Chicago mood among many young people has been one of disenchantment, despair, privatism — and for some, increasing violence.

I have two young legislative assistants on my Congressional staff. Just five years ago one of them was doing voter registration work in a predominantly black county in Southwest Georgia, and the other was in the Peace Corps in Tanzania. It is a commentary on the shifting mood of the younger generation that today both these involvements seem just a trifle quaint.

Where five years ago the response of youth to the failures and weaknesses of American institutions was to get into them and try to change them, to bring them around, many today are either selling out, throwing out, or dropping out — but in any case, *out*. What this means, symbolically and literally, is that for many of our most thoughtful young people it is no longer desirable to be *in*, to be involved in the institutions that govern and shape our common life.

Let us look for a minute at these three typical responses. "Selling out" is hardly what we adults would call it, but young people use the term to mean that someone has compromised his youthful ideals by joining the Establishment. An associate told me of a recent Yale graduate who took his master's degree at the Harvard Business School and then went to work for a leading Wall Street stock brokerage house. When he returned to Yale for a reunion with some of his classmates, he found himself just a little embarrassed to tell them what he was doing — where his counterpart a few years ago would have been bursting with pride.

He had sold out. His embarrassment was real, and what it said was that many of today's brightest students are having a more and more difficult time identifying with institutions which only a short time ago would happily have claimed most of their waking lives.

Dr. Jeffrey K. Hadden, a psychologist at Tulane University, has ventured the opinion that there is a new ethic, a new ideology, emerging among young people in America. He calls it an ethic of privatism. It is true, he feels, that as a whole, young people today are perhaps less hypocritical than their elders. It is true that they have been sensitized somehow to injustice in our society; they are quicker to recognize racism, quicker to see that there are serious things wrong with our country despite the superficial appearance of abundance and prosperity. But at the same time, Dr. Hadden doubts whether the great mass of young people today really feel any heartfelt commitment to the ideals they profess to espouse. He cites statistics from a poll which indicates that some forty-two percent of American students in 1969 believed that middle-class Americans live in largely segregated, all-white neighborhoods and send their children to segregated schools. Yet the same number of students have no other thought than to become part of that same middle-class society they so sharply condemn. They apparently feel scant obligation to do anything about it.

The second typical response of American youth to the failures of our institutions and ideals has been to try to throw them out. What began at the outset of this decade as a non-violent movement, dedicated to righting civil wrongs and integrating our society, became a frustrated and futile thunderhead as the Vietnam war imposed itself on our national conscience and would not move. No longer successfully able to influence national policy or priorities, students turned to protest, confrontation, and the politics of violence. The word "revolution," long a theoretical construct in political science seminars, crept into conversations in college dining halls and dorms. Thwarted and frustrated in the attempt to build or change, the only action left was to destroy.

John Gardner, now Chairman of the Urban Coalition, has observed that an important segment of young people has accepted the view that "man is naturally good, humane, decent, just, and honorable — but that corrupt and wicked institutions have transformed the noble savage into a civilized monster. Destroy the corrupt institutions, they say, and man's native goodness will flower." There isn't anything in history or anthropology to confirm the thesis, though it survives through the generations.

There is a primitivism about this that reminds me of the story from Old Testament history of Samson. He was led into the temple and chained between two of its supporting pillars. In one last desperate display of strength to confound his mocking enemies, he pulled down the pillars and perished there in the ruins of the temple along with his adversaries. Some young radicals today, in an effort to slay the Philistines in our midst, seem prepared to engage in a suicidal act of self-destruction.

It is perhaps too early to gauge the extent and impact of this kind of thinking on American youth. Most talk of revolution, I am convinced, remains hypothetical. But we should not underestimate its potential influence, for the spiritual climate of our times has already been deeply colored by the rhetoric of violence, and where the spirit of violence flourishes, the act, as we have seen, from Santa Barbara to Manhattan, cannot be far behind.

I cannot believe that the answer is suppression. To deny that problems exist, to brand as "trouble-makers" or "outside agitators" those who have given up on traditional modes of reconciling differences, is to miss the point that our society is in trouble, and trying to cover it up will only aggravate the problem. Ultimately, the only thing that will allow our political, social, economic, and cultural institutions to survive in anything like their present form, will be far-reaching change in their structure and operations. We need the kind of reform that will restore a sense of individual worth and meaning to the daily tasks and common relationships upon which our large and complex society must depend.

The third response that seems to be increasingly characteristic among many groups of students and young people is in many ways the most interesting and the most disturbing. It is "dropping out." Faced with mounting problems, the break-down of established order, and the bankruptcy of established social processes, many students have turned inward, shunning society and public life in a search for inner truth and inner peace.

In recent years we have also seen among the young a growing fascination with drugs, acid rock, meditation, and other elements of what we may call an emerging psychedelic culture. "Psychedelic" literally means "mind-manifesting," and thus we find "Homo Psychedelius," the hero of this new life style, engaged in the absorbing activity of exploring inner space.

The emergence of "Homo Psychedelius" has several profound implications for American society and culture. First, there is the sheer uncertainty about the physical effects of drugs on their users.

Our attitudes about the use of drugs may well change as their effects are better documented and studied. I am hardly an expert, but it seems to me worth noting that Dr. Hardin Jones, Professor of Physiology and Medical Physics at the University of California at Berkeley, has said that up to one half of all people between the ages of fifteen and thirty in this country could expose themselves to serious illness or even death within the next five years through the use of drugs. The possibilities of permanent physical damage and even a genetic effect on a future generation are truly frightening.

As a politician who believes that our system of government, though tarnished and creaky, may be the best hope we have for solving our common problems, I am more concerned by the effect that this new culture may have on participation in social and political life. If apathy is setting in on a grand scale among our brightest young people, then in my judgment that represents a more serious threat to American society than talk of revolution.

If instead of getting positively involved in American society, an important segment of our young people are selling out, throwing out, or dropping out, then where do we look to find the answer to this growing malaise that stretches the generation gap and threatens to undermine the foundations of American life? I believe we have to look partly at the institutions under attack, about which I will have more to say in the next chapter, and partly at the unmet needs of these young people themselves, and especially the yearning that many feel to make their lives count for something beyond themselves.

We have seen more and more examples of this in recent years. One has been the tendency for young people to look elsewhere than to business for a career. We have created the Peace Corps, Vista, and an Office of Voluntary Services in the executive office of the President to seek to channel a new breed of public-minded young persons into public service. In 1969 when we were preparing for the battle over the extension of the poverty program, the Director of OEO's Office of Legal Services told me that the Office of Economic Opportunity was getting some of the top students from the most prestigious law schools in the country to volunteer for service in its legal clinics. There they would not command the fees paid by large corporations, but they would enjoy the supreme satisfaction of providing legal assistance to the poor and the disadvantaged, blacks and Mexican-Americans, and poor whites who rarely even understood their rights, let alone had someone to fight for them.

I believe we ought to give priority to a national goal of providing every encouragement to young people to devote some period of their lives, presumably post-high school or college, to assisting an agency, public or private, that is seeking to fulfill some of the unmet social needs of our time. I believe our youth would rise to a challenge such as this, for it seems to me that they understand intuitively, perhaps better than some of their elders, that they will find true meaning only through constructive involvement in the problems and needs, hopes and joys of other people. As young Arlo puts it, "It's only by having no self-gratifying goal that you can ever really fulfill yourself."

But even constructive involvement in the lives of other people is not always enough, and perhaps it would not be amiss at this point to suggest that sometimes we delude ourselves in thinking that good works alone will quell that restlessness of the spirit which is the hallmark of youth. Many young people today, even the most idealistic and committed, are genuinely troubled in spirit and almost desperately searching for someone in whom they can believe, or something that will give their lives meaning. Vincent Canby, in a review of the film "Woodstock," has this to say:

> The great irony of the film is that although the scene does seem incredibly benign, the beauty so often spoken of is really nothing more than a desperate, deeply felt wish, a prayer. "Beautiful!" one little girl says of the festival, and then goes on to tell the interviewer how her sister has disappeared, high on meth, and that she hopes she can find her before Monday because the sister has to appear in court. But it's all "beautiful," she insists, and the scene was, for me, both as moving, and as terrifyingly mindless as a late bulletin from Southeast Asia.

If we as Christians really do believe that Christ is the Way, the Truth, and the Life, then we have never had a greater challenge, responsibility, or opportunity to communicate that message in language that young people can understand.

9
DOES "THE SYSTEM" STILL WORK?

I still carry the vivid memory of that day in January of 1961 when John F. Kennedy was inaugurated the thirty-fifth President of the United States. I had begun my own career as a Congressman just a few days before when I took the oath of office to serve as a Representative from the 16th District of Illinois.

As the young, new president's voice rose and fell in the soaring cadences of that memorable Inaugural Address, I listened intently, completely absorbed by the spell of the occasion. He voiced the conviction that the decade which we were just beginning — the Sixties — would determine whether or not our institutions of democratic government were capable of surviving the challenges which even then had appeared on the near horizon. He foresaw a time of testing and trial which would be unique in the history of our Republic. Although he did not survive to witness the full extent of his prescience, it was a self-fulfilling prophecy, as even the most casual historian of that period now recognizes.

War, racism, revolt bordering on nihilism — these were the great purging tides that washed over us in the Sixties. In each of these situations our time-honored institutions seemed less than adequate or responsive.

Congress, which under the Constitution was given the power to provide for the common defense and to declare war, had permitted our country to become involved in the third most costly war in our history, without the exercise of its constitutional duty to make a solemn Declaration of War. Few accepted the tortured reasoning of Under Secretary of State Nicholas Katzenbach before a Congressional Committee that the Gulf of Tonkin Resolution was the functional equivalent of such a formal declaration as had preceded our entry into World Wars One and Two.

Thus we were plunged into doubt about the very ability of our system of government to prevent a strong-willed President from usurping the power to make war. The passage of the so-called National Commitments Resolution by the United States Senate in 1969 was tacit recognition of these flaws. It sought to reassert Congressional prerogatives in the field of foreign policy and to forbid the commitment of United States troops outside the Continental limits unless by the express sanction of an Act of Congress.

The problem of racism also called into serious question the ability of our institutions to respond to the crisis caused by increasing black and white polarization. Sixteen years after the United States Supreme Court in *Brown v. Board of Education* had ruled that segregated schools were a violation of the United States Constitution, millions of blacks were still attending all-black schools in the South. More than a decade and a half after a clear decision that separate but equal schools did not meet the stern constitutional test of equal protection of the laws, we were still faced with *de facto* segregation in the North, the result of economic factors and discriminatory housing patterns.

The problem of racism in America does not involve merely governmental institutions. There is a failure which looms even larger than that of our legal or administrative machinery: our failure to see a real breakthrough in basic national attitudes toward the problem of race. As yet we have neither a sense of urgency nor a full appreciation of the problem's dimensions. The institutions of our private sector must share responsibility for the failure to bring us together as one nation.

There are some 320,000 churches in our country. Would anyone challenge the assertion that only the tiniest fraction could be called truly integrated? Yet, when the Master said, "Come, all ye who are heavy laden . . .," He was all-inclusive in His outreach. He did not hesitate to minister to the needs of the Samaritan woman, or to the publicans and sinners. Would not Christ sorrow at our lack of compassion and understanding? In the communities of our nation that have been almost ripped apart by racial strife, it is God's people who ought to be asking themselves, "Where have we failed, and what must we do, to bind up the wounds that have opened up in our city?" It is the passivity of many Christians on this issue that I find so deeply disturbing. They simply don't recognize any complicity for conditions that have been festering for many years, nor do they really care to have a part in achieving any solution. If some of our white suburban churches would even sponsor an occasional exchange service with a black congregation in the inner city, this might begin to build that bridge of Christian love and understanding that will have to precede any truly meaningful attempts to break down these attitudes of suspicion, fear, ignorance, and distrust.

There are other institutions in the private sector of our society which are equally culpable. Until very recently, many trade unions have consistently engaged in discriminatory practices designed to keep blacks from joining the ranks of journeymen in the various crafts. Despite some progress, many are still guilty of imposing artificial barriers which keep blacks from competing with whites for the better paying jobs in such fields as the construction industry. Nor can management escape its share of the blame for a national failure to work actively toward a truly integrated society. The extremely low percentage of blacks in white collar jobs is not solely attributable to a lack of qualified people to promote or to place in these positions. Racist attitudes have been exhibited at the managerial level as well.

It was because of the inadequate response of our institutions to war, racism, and a pervasive poverty in the midst of plenty that toward the close of the Sixties the black flag of anarchy became the battle standard of some extremist groups in our society. To call them extremists is not to minimize the threat that they represent. President Nixon was obliged early in 1970 to recommend to the Congress new penal legislation to prevent the bombing and dynamiting of public buildings and the headquarters of giant American corporations. The threat to internal order was very real indeed. The more gloomy in our midst even saw an analogy to the activities of the Algerian terrorists and guerillas during the campaign to rid their country of French rule. Bizarre as the activities of the radical Weatherman faction of the Students for a Democratic Society were, they dramatized the fact that, for some, the answer has become a revolution every bit as cataclysmic as those which shook the world in 1789 and 1917.

This attempted legitimization of violence is based on the belief that our institutions, both public and private, have lost any right to continue to exist because they are part of a system that simply does not work. It is a philosophy of nihilism which has attracted the bored, the disaffected, and the brilliant student as well as the drop-out, the child of affluence as well as the disadvantaged. The spiritual progenitor of many of these modern revolutionaries is Mao Tse Tung, who teaches that power grows out of a gun barrel. The former leader of the Black Panther Party in Illinois, Fred Hampton, who died in a hail of police bullets, left a political testament shortly before his death in the form of an interview with William Braden of the Chicago *Sun Times*. Hampton was quoted as saying, "I think that objectively there is going to be an armed struggle. People have to be armed to have power, you see."

I believe that the motive force behind genuine progress is not the power that grows out of a gun barrel, but the power of the idea that man is a spiritual being. It follows that only as we maximize the opportunities for an expression of that spirit, in a climate free of oppression and discrimination, will we move toward the goal of allowing everyone to achieve his full potential. The Scriptures tell us that "where the Spirit of the Lord is, there is liberty." If we, as Christians, are truly filled with the Spirit, we will seek to do those things that will enlarge the freedom of all our fellowmen.

As we have watched the often inadequate responses of our institutions to the crises thrown up by the turbulent Sixties, many have asked, "Does the system still work? Is American democracy still viable?" A few of the young seem to have concluded already that it is not, and so they rail and raise their fists against "the System" and against "the Establishment," seeking quixotically to bring them crashing down.

As an American and as one who has devoted much of his life to public service, I feel a deep commitment to these institutions, besieged though they be. I still believe in American democracy, not just for the sake of a glorious past, but because I believe it is our only real hope for achieving a truly free and open society in the future. Our democratic institutions may be creaky in spots, they may be in need of some repair, but they have served us well and there is no acceptable alternative system that I can see on the horizon. As Sir Winston Churchill wryly put it, "Democracy is surely the worst form of government except for all the others that have been tried."

But I also believe that we cannot afford simply to take the defensive and become apologists for the status quo. We have to make our democratic institutions relevant anew in each generation, and if the lesson of the Sixties is that these institutions are not adequately meeting the problems our society faces, then we should look for ways in which to make these institutions that we cherish responsive to the demands of a new decade.

As a Congressman, I have been especially concerned about our institutions of government and politics. Many are badly in need of reform if they are to continue to serve the purpose for which they were created. The late Speaker of the House, Sam Rayburn, was said to advise young Congressmen that the way to get along was to go along. Unfortunately, generations of legislators have followed that prescription for success to the point where the dead hand of the past often rules long past the time when sound judgment would dictate otherwise.

The shrine of seniority is one at which many of the leading figures in the House continue to worship, for the obvious reason that this is how they came to assume power in the first place. During the 91st Congress, the Speaker of the House observed his seventy-ninth birthday. Of the twenty-one Committee Chairmen in the House, thirteen were over sixty-five; five were over seventy, and two were over eighty. The role of a Committee Chairman is not just a titular one; he holds real power, and often the virtual power of life and death over important bills. The Chairman has the power to call and to fix the agenda of meetings, decide on witnesses to be heard, and allot time to the members to examine and cross-examine the witnesses. By clever tactics and adroit timing and maneuvering, he can literally frustrate the majority of a Committee at least over a period of time, if not actually for an indefinite period. Therefore the manner of selecting committee chairmen is crucial to the way in which the Congress transacts its business. Today that system is the Seniority System. The oldest member of the committee in point of service becomes chairman, if he is also a member of the majority party. The only exception in recent years involved Adam Clayton Powell, who was formally stripped of his seniority by the Democratic Caucus because of his numerous misdeeds and thereby lost his Chairmanship of the Education and Labor Committee.

The Chairman of one of the committees on which I serve is now into his eighty-first year; he patiently waited until his seventy-fifth year before assuming the reins of the chairmanship. Under the Seniority System, he could not advance until the senior Democrat on the committee, himself an octagenarian, decided to retire or was defeated. The latter event finally occurred, and the Rules Committee then received fresh leadership in the person of seventy-five-year-old William Colmer of Mississippi, a kindly and courtly gentleman of the Old South best known for his tenacious opposition to any and all Civil Rights bills.

The former Chairman of the Rules Committee, Howard A. Smith of Virginia, was also a notorious foe of any Civil Rights bills. "Judge" Smith would simply retire to his farm in Virginia to avoid calling his committee together to grant a rule on a bill so that it could be brought to the floor for a vote. This situation was aggravated by the fact that the committee did not even have a set of standing rules which required the chairman to call a meeting on a fixed day each week. There was a rather cumbersome procedure whereby a majority could serve notice on the chairman and demand that he call a meeting within five days, but it was sometimes difficult even to find the chairman to serve him the notice.

Today the Seniority System is under sustained assault and faces the most serious challenge to its continued existence since it was established more than half a century ago. A recent survey of major American business corporations showed that the average age of the president or chief executive offices was only fifty-seven. I believe this fact alone provides ample reason to consider junking the present geriatrically-oriented system in favor of a more democratic procedure such as electing committee chairmen from among the most skilled and experienced members on a particular committee who belong to the majority party.

We need to reform the institutions of our society in both the governmental and non-governmental sectors. Let us lower the voting age to eighteen and bring participatory democracy to millions of young people. Let us overhaul the archaic machinery of Congress and make it more responsive to the wishes of the people. Let us urge the 320,000 churches and hundreds of thousands of other voluntary associations within the private sector of American society to cooperate in a new program started by the Nixon Administration to mobilize volunteers to attack a myriad of social problems. The truly distinctive contribution that the Christian can make to this effort is his willingness to obey the commandment, "Thou shalt love thy neighbor as thyself." And who is my neighbor? He is anyone in need, regardless of color, education, background or status in life.

John Gardner, former Secretary of Health, Education and Welfare, has said that a civilization is not something like the pyramids which can endure simply by standing there as a mute memorial to the past. It must be re-created by each generation of thinking, believing, and caring men and women. As Christians we must believe enough and care enough to follow the example of Nehemiah, who left the ease and comforts of King Artaxerxes' court to rebuild the walls of the Holy City, Jerusalem, and to lead the moral and religious rebirth of his people. This is the kind of faith and the kind of spirit that must move us as Christians to join in repairing and rebuilding the battered walls of the nation which we cherish and seek to preserve.

I believe that if there is a solution to the present crisis, it is to be found in the words Joshua employed on the occasion of his farewell to the assembled tribes of Israel, "Choose you this day whom ye will serve . . ." (Joshua 24:15). Just as in Joshua's day, we have a generation which has been given ". . . a land for which ye did not labour, and cities which ye built not, and ye dwell in them; of the vineyards and oliveyards which ye planted not do ye eat" (Joshua 24:13).

We have inherited a great land, one conceived in liberty and dedicated to the proposition that men are equal in God's sight. We can maintain and extend that liberty and equality if we renew in spirit the historic covenant which, early in our history, found expression in the Mayflower Compact:

> In the Name of God, Amen. We whose names are underwritten . . . do by these presents solemnly and mutually in the presence of God, and one of another, covenant and combine ourselves together into a civil body politic, for our better ordering and preservation and furtherance of the ends aforesaid; and by virtue hereof to enact, constitute and frame such just and equal laws, ordinances, acts, constitutions, and offices, from time to time, as shall be thought most meet and convenient for the general good of the Colony: unto which we promise all due submission and obedience.

So long as we are able to covenant ourselves into a civil body politic, and to frame and administer such just and equal laws as will contribute to the general good, I believe American democracy will survive and flourish.

But we must remember that the crisis John F. Kennedy foresaw for the decade of the Sixties confronts us anew as we stand on the threshold of a new decade. The question of the relevancy and responsiveness of our democratic institutions to problems even more staggering than he foresaw is still to be decided. For as the late President himself said, "Those who make non-violent change impossible make violent change inevitable."

10
PUTTING GOVERNMENT IN THE HANDS OF THE PEOPLE

We have seen how war, racism, and revolution led to a "shaking of the foundations" in the 1960's and called in question the ability of our institutions to respond to newly developing crises. But the decade of the Sixties also raised the specter of another crisis, less dramatic in its impact than the portent of revolution perhaps, but in the long run even more ominous.

When Richard Nixon became our thirty-seventh President, the decade was ending. He spoke in his Inaugural Address of a "crisis of the spirit" and of a "ragged spirit." It is scarcely necessary to recount the recent history of our times that impelled him to make that judgment. Overwhelmed by the onrushing development of our own technology and what Professor Will Herberg refers to as the "massification" of our society, we are discovering that we have paid a heavy price for what passes for progress. I am reminded of the words of the prophet Isaiah, "Woe unto them that join house to house, that lay field to field, till there be no place, that they may be placed alone in the midst of the earth" (Isaiah 5:8). The heart cry of modern man is often one that bespeaks the spirit of loneliness, even as he walks amid canyons formed by towering skyscrapers and finds himself tossed on a surging tide of humanity like a cork bobbing on the waters.

It is this very massification of Russian society that has produced Soviet Man. Save for a few aberrations like Grigorenko or Solzhenitsyn, Soviet citizens seem willing to subordinate their individual egos to the disciplined requirements of the state planners. Even their art forms are designed not to express individual ideas or temperament, but to serve some preordained notion of what culture should be in a classless society which has been liberated from mere bourgeois tendencies.

How do we maintain a spirit of individual worthiness in each man and woman when our lives have become so specialized, functionalized, and compartmentalized? It seems to me that we must nurture a revival

78

of that spirit or run the risk of witnessing the continued erosion of freedom. Any large and increasingly complex society is prone to massification, but in recent years American institutions have seemed particularly and increasingly susceptible to this trend.

In its simplest dress, massification contributes to a diminishing concern for people as individuals. Corporate growth, big government, an exploding population, computerized social management, and the rising crescendo of technological change — all these trends have combined to make us feel that the institutions which do so much to shape our lives are less and less responsive to individual efforts, individual problems, individual hopes and fears.

The sense prevails that somehow we have lost control, that the great corporations, government agencies, universities, foundations and television networks that claim so much of our lives are rushing mindlessly into the future, immune from all our attempts to restore reflection, sanity, and purpose to our national life. "We no longer matter" — such is the view of those who have given in to gloom.

And while I do not share this view, I believe the problem of bigness — aimless, impersonal, uncontrolled — can no longer be dismissed or ignored by those of us who really care about the kind of society we are building in America today. We have to find ways in which to make our institutions, and ourselves, more aware of the human dimension in our common life, and more responsive to the real needs of individual people.

The mass gatherings we have seen in recent years, especially those organized by young people, impress me as eloquent testimony to this growing crisis of the spirit. Some 400,000 young people gathered at Woodstock, New York, in August, 1969, not so much to express dissent as to draw some human strength and personal meaning from each other. Some observers even said the Moratorium Day marches that same year in cities from Washington to San Francisco were more communal than political. It was almost as if people came together in such masses out of a deep well of loneliness.

I wonder if people are not seeking a common purpose, a common goal, and a common identity because they feel they lead such impersonal, fragmented, and isolated lives. This seems strange, and maybe inconsistent, when we stop to reflect that today more than seventy percent of the total population of our country is concentrated in cities. The process of urbanization goes on apace, and yet despite the fact that we are crowded together, as David Riesman says, it is a lonely crowd. More and more we are fighting this growing depersonalization and trying somehow to reach out beyond ourselves. In the great onrush of modern life, we literally brush past people without having any kind of contact, or without making any communion with them.

This point was brought home to me with telling force as I was driving home from work one evening in Washington. I was on the Southwest Freeway, a busy crowded highway. As I came to a little traffic island, I saw a young black woman walking aimlessly back and forth. I could see that she was crying. I stopped for a red light, leaned out the window, and asked her what was wrong. She spoke with a foreign accent and I could hardly understand her. Finally, I gathered that she was lost.

The man in the car behind me began to honk his horn, so I shouted a few directions through the window and sped away. I went for a mile or so, and then I grew a little ashamed of myself. I thought, "What a horrible thing, to let somebody scare you off just because he's leaning on his horn. Maybe that woman is in trouble."

So I turned around and went back. Sure enough, there she was, still walking around in a daze. I asked her to get into the car and tried to find out what the problem was. I found out she was from Guiana, was working in Washington, and had gotten into an argument with a cab driver because she thought he was taking her to the wrong place. He promptly dumped her out and there she was, lost and unable to get another cab.

When I finally got all the details straightened out, I took her to a hotel where she could get a bus. As I thought about it, this seemed to be just a small example of how we get so busy, so hemmed in by all the pressures that mount on every side, that there isn't any time left even to observe the basic civilities and courtesies that were more habitual in earlier times. I think this is a disturbing measure of the kind of times in which we live.

Not long ago *Time* magazine featured a cover story entitled "Why Nothing Seems to Work Any More." I think the title captured a growing feeling of frustration among Americans of all ages who have simply had it up to here with the breakdowns that seem increasingly endemic in our society. Teachers, postal workers, firemen, and garbage collectors are on strike; the telephone snarl is getting worse; highways are clogged, airports strikebound, and trains late; lines are lengthening and prices rising for the simplest services. Where will it all end? Nothing we do seems to help, and in frustration we long for earlier, simpler times.

The rise of bigness — and the loss of purpose and control, depersonalization, and breakdown that have accompanied it — have had a tremendously enervating effect on the American spirit, and in my judgment have contributed greatly to the more dramatic failures of our institutions that we noted in the last chapter. As our great corporations, government agencies, and other institutions have grown beyond the reach of individuals, they have become faceless concentrations of power too unwieldy to control. The growing facelessness of our corporate life has had a corresponding effect on our personal lives, and we have gradually learned to treat other human beings as nameless consumers, numbers, bodies, things to be used or ignored, but rarely treated with personal warmth or concern. As the final chapter in the process, the things we have manufactured to add convenience to this impersonal style of life have conspired against us and added to our headaches instead of our ease of mind.

If there is a remedy for this situation, it seems to me it must lie at least partly in new attempts to decentralize our institutions, to break them down wherever possible into more manageable, more responsive units. In city planning this would mean giving greater emphasis to smaller, more cohesive neighborhood communities. In education it might mean building more schools and reducing the size of classes. In business it might mean providing incentives for the little man and trying to check the unbridled growth of conglomerates and corporations, whose size no longer reflects economies of scale but merely the desire for a bigger balance sheet. In the media, the attempt to decentralize power might mean encouraging the growth of local networks and checking the growth of monopoly power in the press.

But it is in government that I believe the opportunities are greatest for decentralizing power, restoring local initiative, and increasing individual participation. And in this regard, I believe President Nixon's proposals for a "New Federalism" constitute one of the most significant initiatives of his administration. It would be premature to predict that these programs will reverse, by themselves, the trend toward aimless bigness that we have described. Yet as a witness to what can be accomplished with purpose and imagination, they must rank as proposals of the first importance, and among the most farsighted of any Chief Executive in this century.

We are beginning to plan for the bicentennial celebration of our Declaration of Independence in 1976. Although we still think of ourselves as a young nation, more than 180 years have passed since the architects of our Constitution labored through the hot summer of 1787 to fashion the document which represents our fundamental law. The true genius of the system of government devised by those fifty-five remarkable men, whom we call the Founding Fathers, was that it provided for a balanced distribution of power among the several states, and between the states and the new central government.

We call that system "federalism." Drawing on their knowledge and understanding of political philosophers from Plato and Aristotle to Locke, Rousseau, Montesquieu, and Paine, the writers of our Constitution fashioned a system which gave necessary power to the national government in such matters as foreign policy and taxation, yet reserved to the states responsibility for shaping local institutions and meeting local needs. The Founding Fathers were determined to avoid a future lapse into the authoritarianism so characteristic of European government of that era. Yet the sorry experiences we had suffered under the Articles of Confederation made them equally determined to construct a framework for government that would clothe the new President, Congress, and Supreme Court with sufficient power to preserve the delicate fabric of the new Republic.

For a century and a half, through sectional strife and civil war, that framework was preserved. But in the crisis years of the 1930's much of the balance originally written into the Constitution was upset as power became increasingly centralized in Washington. Now as we enter the final third of the twentieth century, we find spreading dissatisfaction with the manner in which the federal government has exercised the vast powers it has accumulated. Here the generation gap closes. Both young and old profess disillusionment with the inability of government to deal more efficiently and efficaciously with the delivery of health care under Medicare and Medicaid, with burgeoning welfare rolls in a time of great prosperity, with the increasing involvement of federal bureaucrats in everything from farm problems to social security and the increasing inability of state and local governments to finance their needs and meet their responsibilities.

Unquestionably the Nixon Administration rode to power on the crest of the wave of resentment against the war in Vietnam. However, it would be a great mistake to discount the importance of this generalized discontent with the malfunctioning of the federal bureaucracy in many different areas.

In an address to the nation on 8 August 1969, President Nixon addressed himself to this problem and offered the proposals which have become known as "the New Federalism":

> My purpose is to present a new set of reforms — a new set of proposals — a new and drastically different approach to the way in which government cares for those in need, and to the way the responsibilities are shared between the state and federal government. I have chosen to do so in a direct report to the people because these proposals call for public decisions of the first importance; because they represent a fundamental change in the nation's approach to one of its most pressing social problems, and because, quite deliberately, they also represent the first major reversal of the trend toward ever more centralization of government in Washington, D.C. After a third of a century of power flowing from the people and the states to Washington, it is time for a New Federalism, in which power, funds, and responsibility will flow from Washington to the states and to the people.
>
> During last year's election campaign, I often made a point that touched a responsive chord wherever I traveled.
>
> I said that this nation became great, not because of what the government did for people, but because of what people did for themselves.

The New Federalism — a package of three proposals embodying revenue sharing, welfare reform, and manpower retraining — is aimed at strengthening the roots of our federal system by re-invigorating state and local governments. In government, money is power, and today the mightiest fiscal tool is the federal income tax. States and local governments have relied largely on property taxes, sales and excise taxes, and a flat or only mildly progressive tax on incomes as sources of revenue. But demands for new and improved public services have totally outstripped their ability to finance these programs.

The President has proposed a revenue-sharing program that would, if adopted, provide a five billion dollar fund by 1976, which would be distributed on a formula basis to states and local municipalities. I believe revenue sharing should be adopted as a means of strengthening the ability of these units of government to deal with what are often essentially local rather than national problems.

In welfare reform, the thrust of the New Federalism is to give states more resources and broader responsibilities for shaping their own programs. This does not mean a total renunciation of federal responsibility in welfare; if implemented, it will mean the use of federal money to equalize state payments to needy families and thus eliminate the gross discrepancies which now exist. Even allowing for regional differences in the cost of living, the differences between payments for the support of dependent children in some Southern states and the payments made in Northern and Western states is truly shocking. They range from $263.00 per month for a mother with three children in one state, down to $39.00 a month in a state with the lowest payments.

By insisting on a minimum for payments to both the working and the non-working poor, the federal government, in my opinion, asserts its interest in preserving the family unit. Under the old system, the father often had an incentive to desert rather than remain as head of the family, for by abandoning his wife and children, they became eligible for welfare, whereas payments were not made when there was a working father as head of the household. As a result, the problem of the "runaway pappy" has become a national scandal. I do not want to suggest that this reform in welfare laws will automatically solve all of our problems in this area, but it should help to make them more manageable. This reform would be combined with a requirement that welfare recipients, with some exceptions (those with children under six, or those who are disabled), register for work and also for job training.

Another New Federalism proposal contemplates the complete overhaul of all these manpower training services, on which, in a recent year, we spent several billions of dollars. It would provide for gradually decentralizing their administration so that states and municipalities could run programs tailored to the demands of the labor market in their particular section or area of the country.

Not all of the proposals which I have outlined have met with universal approbation. Some have stirred opposition, particularly the welfare reform proposal, which for the first time would make the working poor eligible to receive certain benefits as long as their income remains below an officially designated poverty level. There are those who raise the specter of the free bread and circuses which marked the declining days of Rome, and they profess to see a similarity in this attempt to assist the poor.

I disagree. When Christ was moved by the hunger of the multitudes who came to hear Him, there were those among His own disciples who urged that He send them away to find their own food. Jesus rejected their suggestion, and in reliance upon the providence of His heavenly Father, performed the familiar miracle of the loaves and the fishes. He did not do this to curry favor with the crowd, or to win their support for His cause. Quite to the contrary, John in his gospel has recorded that after performing this miracle, Christ realized that the crowd desired to carry Him off literally on their shoulders and make Him their king. And so He retired from among them and communed with His Father (John 6:15).

It would be futile and perhaps foolish to deny that there are those who will see in this new welfare program the opportunity to bid for votes from the class to be benefitted. Not all politicians will be able to follow the example of the Master and resist the blandishments of the crowd. But without this reform, four million more Americans will be added to the welfare rolls by 1975, at a cost of almost eleven billion dollars a year. I think the alternative of continuing down the same path which has led to the present disillusionment with the processes of democratic government is far more bleak. The cynicism and despair arising out of our failure to deal effectively with the problems of the poor has led to what James Reston called "the new pessimism." What makes it so profoundly alarming is that it is a pessimism which calls into question the very ability of our institutions of government to cope with the present crisis.

I believe the New Federalism can be the road to a restored faith in American Democracy among young and old, black and white, rich and poor. It can do this by bringing government a little closer to the people whom it is designed to serve. If we can replace the image in the average citizen's mind of an anonymous and faceless bureaucracy, with a feeling that many people at all levels of government are working together in a cooperative effort to cure the ills of our society, we will have given new meaning and new stature to representative democracy. Massification will not be reversed overnight, but in the New Federalism we now have a model approach which I hope will be used in other areas to give individual citizens increasing participation and control over the decisions and initiatives which so greatly affect their daily lives.

ISSUES

The institutions of our society provide the framework within which we carry on our daily life and work. I have tried to show why I believe this framework must be not only strong but flexible, in order to provide for orderly, non-violent change through processes that reflect credit, not just on the Founding Fathers who wrote our Constitution, but on the wisdom of our own people today.

I would like to turn now from institutions to issues. The next six chapters are devoted to what I believe will be among the most critical issues of the Seventies — Vietnam and foreign policy; the use of atomic power for war and peace; the scourge of racism; poverty; crime; and the environment. The decisions we make on these issues will, in my opinion, have much to do with whether or not our institutions survive in anything like their present form.

11
VIETNAM
AND
BEYOND

In this and succeeding chapters I propose to discuss some of the most urgent problems confronting America as we enter the new decade of the 1970's. What I say about these issues must be considered in the light of the foregoing chapters, where I have tried to make my basic principles clear.

There is no need to explain why I have chosen to start with Vietnam. I wish I could avoid it, because I have no easy solutions. But I do want to sketch the general principles I believe we should keep in mind in seeking a solution to this disastrous war.

Robert C. Good, our former ambassador to Zambia, said in an article in the *Washington Post* (7 September 1969):

> . . . Disillusionment creates a receptivity for new illusions; and as a people we are not beyond the danger of replacing one oversimplification for another . . . . Take Vietnam, for example. The war has become a source of unrest so deep in our national life that we are probably expecting too much from ultimate disengagement. We have told ourselves over and over again that it has distorted our priorities, played havoc with our image abroad, radicalized our students, inflamed black militants, and given rise to feelings of national guilt in sensitive sectors of our population. All these things are in a measure true. The domestic consequences have overwhelmed the foreign and we must withdraw . . . . But the method and the terms of our disengagement from Vietnam will also deeply affect both our policy problems and our national life. That is why we should be patient while this Administration attempts an honorable compromise.

By contrast, a minister of my acquaintance, although not of my constituency, recently wrote me in this vein: "Unless you immediately and publicly condemn the present Administration's policy in Vietnam as morally indefensible, you are as guilty of sin as those men who, 125 years ago, silently stood by and said nothing about the horror of human slavery in the South." This letter was written at a time when the Nixon Administration had declared its policy of withdrawal was irreversible and had already announced troop withdrawals totaling 115,000 men.

I believe that our involvement in Vietnam constitutes the most tragic error in diplomatic and military policy in our nation's history. As one who participated in government during the years in which this error was being compounded, I am willing to accept my share of personal culpability for a lack of greater prescience as to where those errors would take us. The fact is that, small step by small step, we blundered into "the endless bog" which the Japanese call the dreaded "dorunuma."

I believe we must now take responsibility before history for leading our own people and the people of Vietnam into this dorunuma of suffering. None of us can or should escape the knowledge that our errors of judgment probably caused more death and destruction, and, in the long run, brought less stability and security not only to Vietnam but to our country as well, than would have been the case if we had never intervened. We will rightly bear the scars of this tragedy for a generation, and some of us for the rest of our lives.

But the charge of moral guilt I cannot accept — either for myself or for those others in my country's highest councils who made these errors in the earnest belief that they were trying to avert suffering rather than cause it. This is not, I believe, simply stubborn human pride — for our pride has already been abased in the failure of our efforts to achieve a military victory. We are guilty, not of intentional evil, but of blindness, and specifically of an inability to perceive the difference between a situation such as World War Two, in which America's security itself required a foreign military effort, and a situation such as Vietnam in which the threat to our own security was indirect at best, and in which our power should have been employed in an entirely different manner if at all.

Nor do I accept the charge that some would bring, that our involvement in Vietnam stemmed from venal motives such as economic gain or political imperialism. Our country has lost untold resources and lives in the last decade in Southeast Asia, and at home because of our involvement there. Our leaders believed that an American commitment in Vietnam was necessary to contain the spread of Communism, which, once ensconced in this area, could provide a threat to the peace of the world, and hence the security of the United States. In retrospect, it may be perfectly justifiable to examine and even demolish the validity of that premise, but again, I believe we err if we confuse bad judgment with corrupt motives.

I have sought to confront head-on the issue of alleged moral guilt because the lessons and scars of Vietnam will weigh on our minds and hearts for some time to come. With all the tragedy this war has brought, it would be even more tragic if the wrong lessons were learned and the scars reopened. America is a young nation, and we have traditionally approached foreign involvements with that blend of innocence and quixotic idealism that is peculiar to youth, believing that because we mean well, everything will come out all right in the end. In Vietnam, we have been taught that this is not inevitably so. I would suggest that instead of beating our breasts and withdrawing into the sand like the proverbial ostrich, we should take to heart the lesson that all countries, including our own, are fallible and capable of errors with tragic consequences. Then we will have learned what is perhaps the most important lesson possible for a young nation thrust into world leadership by virtue of its power and its hold on the imagination of men, and in the process we will have gone a long way toward growing up.

One of the tests of that lesson will be whether we turn to the task of reconstruction and rehabilitation with the same vigor we showed in prosecuting the war in the first place. But for now, our efforts must be devoted to disengagement and extrication. Those with a fondness for medical analogies suggest that since Vietnam has become a cancer destroying not only the body, but the very soul of America, we must cut it out. But how do you remove the images of war from the mind of a people, particularly if withdrawal is so abrupt as to constitute clear evidence of ignominy and defeat? It cannot be performed as neatly as a surgical excision. There is a type of surgery so radical that it scars the patient with a trauma of its own, quite apart from that of the disease which the surgery was designed to cure. We could well be scarred by a new isolationism which would reject not only military adventurism, but the kind of responsible cooperation in world affairs required of a great nation.

With a great majority of the American people now convinced that the war in Vietnam was a mistake, it no longer requires political courage to counsel immediate and unilateral withdrawal. What may require courage is the willingness not only to admit that our military involvement in Vietnam was a mistake, but to pursue a course of withdrawal that does not produce trauma with more permanent effects than that already caused by this war.

An unwelcome concomitant could be an enervating effect on the American psyche so severe that we would be unable to address ourselves to the very considerable challenges at home. I do not wish to conjure up imaginary ghosts to haunt us at a time when we need to bring our critical faculties to bear on severe domestic problems. However, history does record that it has often been at a moment of psychological defeat that a nation has surrendered its destiny to some strong man who has promised to restore national purpose and confidence.

If it is now clear that we followed the wrong strategy in getting into Vietnam, then it would be doubly tragic to compound the error by following the wrong strategy in getting out. Strategy consists of a series of planned and coordinated moves in the pursuit of an unrealized objective. Our objective, the restoration of peace both at home and in Southeast Asia, will require a planned and coordinated political, diplomatic, and military effort.

In my judgment, our future policy in Vietnam should be based on the following premises:

We do not seek a military solution in Vietnam. We seek an orderly withdrawal of American troops and a de-escalation of the fighting. We will allow neither Hanoi nor Saigon to dictate the terms of that withdrawal, and we will neither attempt nor accept a precipitate withdrawal. It is not too late to invoke the humanity which we did not always display earlier in prosecuting the war. A pell-mell rush for the beaches could result in the indiscriminate slaughter of those left behind, a moral question we cannot ignore. President Nixon has set and begun a course of orderly withdrawal.

While I hope conditions will merit an acceleration of this policy, we must allow the President necessary latitude and flexibility. It would be unwise to freeze the President into a fixed withdrawal schedule when conditions are so subject to change. Only he is in the best position to fix the timetable, given the existing diplomatic and military developments.

I am not counseling a policy that would allow the Communists to take over country after country. If we now abdicate completely our responsibilities in Vietnam, there might be severe political repercussions that would put world peace even further beyond our reach. But while we have proven the Communists could not defeat American fighting men in Vietnam, we have also proven our own inability to win an essentially political, anti-guerilla war on foreign soil.

By pursuing a more restrained policy in the future, and by refusing to intervene unilaterally in situations like Vietnam, we are not necessarily turning the world over to the Communists. There must be a middle course for America in world affairs, a course that steers clear of the extremes of isolationism and military interventionism.

There are two moods running at cross-currents in our society. One is marked by a sense of fatalism, absurdity, and helplessness, or what some call the "new pessimism." But there is also another mood, a pragmatic "new optimism." This latter spirit is the one that must prevail; we must translate that spirit into a realistic set of policies for the future.

What should be America's role in the world tomorrow? Should we withdraw completely from the international arena and leave the world to its own devices while we concentrate on our own domestic needs? Or should we somehow continue to exercise our responsibilities as the biggest and richest nation in the world?

I believe we have a moral obligation to make some contribution to peace and development in the world. We do not need to impose our will on other nations by military means. We do not need to package our concepts of development and force them on other nations. But, in my judgment, we can and should pursue a constructive and creative internationalism that will promote world peace and development.

The United States cannot play world policeman. President Nixon recognized as much when he enunciated the Guam Doctrine, which has since become a cornerstone of his Administration's foreign policy. He outlined this new, low-profile posture in the 1970 State of the Union Message, when he said:

> Neither the defense nor the development of other nations can be exclusively or primarily an American undertaking. The nations of each part of the world should assume the primary responsibility for their well-being. We shall be faithful to our treaty commitments, but we shall reduce our involvement and our presence in other nations' affairs. To insist that other nations play a role is not a retreat from responsibility; it is a sharing of responsibility. The result of this new policy has been not to weaken our alliances, but to give them new life, new strength, a new sense of common purpose.

As we look beyond Vietnam, I would hope America will continue in its role as a Pacific power, but by maintaining an off-shore rather than a continental presence in Southeast Asia. Japan's role in the Asian community should and will be expanded. President Nixon has also taken some hopeful initiatives to improve relations with Peking. It seems to me that one of the major foreign policy tests of the Seventies will be our success in normalizing relations with China and peacefully bringing it into the community of nations. Much of this effort must depend on China's relations with her own Asian neighbors, for as President Nixon has said, "Our most effective contribution will be to support Asian initiatives in an Asian framework."

The Guam Doctrine applies as well to our relations with Africa and Latin America, where our most effective contributions will be to support African and Latin American initiatives in their own framework. The Action for Progress program announced by the President in October, 1969, signals a basic change in policy toward our neighbors to the south. Rather than a paternalistic relationship under the predominating influence of the United States, it calls for a more mature partnership of equals. As the President said in his speech before the Inter-American Press Association,

> For years we in the United States have pursued the illusion that we could remake continents. Conscious of our wealth and technology, seized by the force of our good intentions, driven by our habitual impatience, remembering the dramatic success of the Marshall Plan in postwar Europe, we have sometimes imagined that we knew what was best for everybody else and that we could and should make it happen. But experience has taught us better. It has taught us that economic and social development is not an achievement of one nation's foreign policy but something deeply rooted in each nation's own traditions . . . .

Again in Europe the Nixon Administration is shifting the emphasis from American domination to genuine partnership, in response to the evident progress of European political and economic development. The Nixon doctrine applied to Europe means that matters such as European unity are basically the concern of Europeans and should not be subordinated to American interests. The winds of change are beginning to blow across the Continent, and I believe we may soon see the day when tensions between Eastern and Western Europe are eased and trade and cultural contacts increased, and when our own military presence on the Continent can be correspondingly reduced.

The Vietnam war has forced us to re-examine our commitments around the globe, and we are left to conclude that, at least in military terms, we are dangerously overextended. We are not prepared to assume a major share of the fighting in all conflicts involving our allies. But to admit that America cannot be policeman to the world will not automatically bring an end to international conflicts; it may, in fact, actually increase their frequency. If we completely dismantle the protective umbrella we have offered to so many free world nations, they will be left in a very vulnerable position. The vacuum would be dangerous.

This vacuum must be filled with some responsible alternatives to American police power. We must begin to think in terms of promoting and fostering regional defense mechanisms capable of dealing with external threats without the need for American intervention. We must promote the peace-keeping functions of the United Nations.

The United Nations was originally created for the purpose of maintaining peace and collective security. Yet it has deteriorated to little more than an international debating society. I have joined with other members of the House and Senate in urging that the Secretary of State give greater consideration to strengthening the peace-keeping functions of the United Nations as a vital arm of our own foreign policy.

Peace is contingent on a number of different conditions as they actually exist in the world, and the impoverished condition of the "third" world is hardly conducive to peace and stability. In the final section of this volume we will have more to say about the widening gap between the haves and the have-nots. This trend will produce disastrous consequences, if something is not done to correct it. We not only have a moral obligation to help our less fortunate neighbors, we have an obligation from the simple standpoint of self-preservation. If we continue to neglect these problems, they will soon be knocking at our own back door; it will then be too late for a peaceful solution.

The answer lies not so much in unilateral American assistance as in a multilateral approach with an emphasis on fostering the kind of development that will preserve a nation's independence and promote its self-reliance. The United Nations could serve as the primary focal point for this kind of assistance. This may not at first be politically palatable to the American people, but in the long run I believe such an approach would be in the best interests of America, since political and economic development of this kind will insure greater stability and peace in the world.

12
THE ARMS RACE AND THE ATOM

In his great epic *Paradise Lost*, the blind poet John Milton describes a furious battle in the heavens between Satan's rebel angels and the forces of good led by the Archangel Michael. In the first day's battle Satan's legions are put to flight, and that night as they regroup to plan the next day's assault, the Prince of Darkness says:

> Weapons more violent, when next we meet,
> May serve to better us, and worse our foes,
> Or equal what between us made the odds,
> In nature none . . .

Satan then produces the world's first field guns:

> . . . hollow Engines long and round
> Thick-rammed, at th'other bore with touch of fire . . .
> Such implements of mischief as shall dash
> To pieces, and o'erwhelm whatever stands
> Adverse, that they shall fear we have disarmed
> The Thunderer of his only dreaded bolt.

Convinced of victory, Satan's hosts march into battle the next day and their great engines of war spread havoc among Michael's angels. But the good angels, not to be outdone, fall back on the ultimate weapon. They tear up the very hills of heaven and cast them against the forces of darkness.

Then Satan's legions, those unburied still, begin to imitate their foes:

> So Hills amid the Air encounter'd Hills
> Hurl'd to and fro with jaculations dire,

until God the Father has to call His own Son to cast the rebel angels down and end the war in heaven, lest

> . . . . in perpetual fight they needs must last
> Endless, and no solution will be found . . . .

96

I believe there is a lesson here for us: once an arms race reaches the stage at which both sides have recourse only to ultimate weapons, then only Divine intervention will insure our survival on this planet in any form of organized society in the event of a nuclear exchange.

From talks with many people across this country and abroad, I have been forced to conclude that many have no conception either of the dimensions of folly building up in our race for nuclear arms or the peril we court in allowing it to continue. Whether expressed in terms of the percentage of our Gross National Product, or in terms of absolute dollars, the present burden imposed on the world by competition for heavier and more sophisticated weaponry is appalling. According to the United States Arms Control and Disarmament Agency, world military spending reached 200 billion dollars at the end of the last decade. This represented more than two years total income for the ninety-three developing countries in which more than two-thirds of the world's entire population lives. Spending on armaments increased forty-four percent just in the last five years of the Sixties. During this period the world's military budgets took as much public money as was spent by all governments on all forms of public education and health care. If these trends continue during the Seventies, the world will be spending more than 300 billion dollars annually for arms by 1980. This would be equal to the value of all the tangible wealth of the United States at the present time — all our homes, factories, highways, minerals, and other real assets.

It is not just the economic burden of the arms race that should make reasonable men shudder in disbelief. Since the first mushroom cloud appeared in the heavens high over the desert floor at Alamagordo, New Mexico, we have had the potential of rendering large portions of this planet, perhaps even the entire earth, as uninhabitable as it became in the time of Noah. Unfortunately, even that comparison does not accurately describe the horror of a nuclear exchange. For in the Book of Genesis, we are told that the waters prevailed upon the earth one hundred and fifty days (Genesis 7:24). Nuclear physicists assure us that the radiological contamination which would follow in the aftermath of thermonuclear war would persist for many years.

In testimony before the Senate Foreign Relations Committee, on 16 March 1970, Marshall D. Shulman, Director of the Russian Institute at Columbia University, summarized our dilemma:

> The Soviet Union and the United States have a common enemy —
> the strategic arms race. Can anyone doubt the proposition that both

countries would be better off, and more secure, if the strategic balance could be maintained at lower levels? And yet, the upward spiral continues, independent of will or reason. The problem is, where and how to initiate the process of checking and then reversing this upward spiral.

The answer is full of technical complexities, but it is fundamentally a political problem. If the will exists to reverse the present senseless trend, ways can be found to solve the technical obstacles. If the will does not exist, or is not strong enough, any technical rationalization will suffice as an epitaph.

It is not a question of trust: the level of mistrust is too high in both directions for that. The real question is whether reasonable men on each side can be brought to recognize and act upon their own rational self-interest.

Former Secretary of Defense Robert S. McNamara once estimated that 400 one-megaton warheads would be sufficient to wipe out three-fourths of the entire industrial base of the Soviet Union and decimate one-third of its population, or approximately 75 million people. At the end of 1970, both the United States and Russia will each have more than 1,000 Minuteman-type missiles, each carrying atomic warheads (the Russian SS-9's having a 25 megaton warhead). In addition, each side has nuclear submarines capable of launching ICBM's and a long range bomber fleet. There is no longer any doubt that each side has stockpiled literally thousands of nuclear devices capable of destroying the other many times over. Yet the mad momentum of this nuclear competition continues amid fear and suspicion that newer and even deadlier weapons will be developed and deployed as part of an increasingly sinister scenario. As if this were not enough, a bellicose and intransigent Red China is busy in Sinkiang Province developing its own nuclear capability.

Toward the end of the Johnson Administration, public concern over the spiralling arms race focused on a proposed new defensive missile system, intended to provide an additional deterrent against possible missile attack by either Communist China or the Soviet Union. Originally called Sentinel, it became known as Safeguard under the Nixon Administration; in the press it is commonly known as ABM, for anti-ballistic missile system. Controversy swirled around the ABM at many levels, political, military, and technical. Proponents of the ABM argued that it was essential to American security in light of increased Soviet and Chinese offensive capabilities. Opponents maintained that on the contrary, it would upset the present delicate "balance of terror," that it was not necessary to American security, and that scientific studies had raised grave questions about whether the ABM would even work as it was intended to.

Knowledgeable, responsible men were divided on this issue. The debate reached its climax in the summer of 1969, when the Senate of the United States approved by two votes the President's request to begin deploying Safeguard missiles. Thus a powerful new defensive weapon has been added to the arsenal of American nuclear arms.

But at the same time that the debate over ABM reached its peak, the American public was becoming aware of a new, probably destabilizing, and potentially far more ominous development in the nuclear arms race. I refer to MIRV, an acronym which stands for Multiple Independently Targetable Re-entry Vehicle. In this weapons system, the portion of the ballistic missile which re-enters the earth's atmosphere after its transcontinental journey is, in effect a bus. Its passengers are a cluster of hydrogen warheads which are capable of responding to command and control to be launched against separate targets.

The quantum jump in the arms race which the introduction and deployment of the MIRV will bring about is patently clear. If each Minuteman missile is retrofitted to include three to five warheads, and we do the same thing to our forty-one Polaris submarines, each with sixteen missiles aboard, we have added additional thousands of nuclear weapons to our stockpile. The Soviets will respond in kind, and we are off to the races again — except that this is one race no one can ever truly win. We can only escalate the grim possibility that somewhere, during this process of building our stock of nuclear chips higher and higher, catastrophe will finally overtake us and a nuclear exchange will occur.

"Balance of terror" is the phrase that we offhandedly use to describe the present stalemate. But in a period of asymmetry or imbalance which could develop as we race toward deployment of this new system, we risk a sudden determination by our adversary that the balance will soon be upset, to his disadvantage. It is precisely at this moment that he may fatalistically decide that it is better to launch a first strike than suffer this impending disadvantage.

It was for this reason that I joined in leading a fight in the ninety-first Congress to secure passage of a resolution recommending to the

President that he propose a mutual moratorium on the testing and deployment of MIRV's by the United States and the Soviet Union.

Although nearly one-quarter of the membership of the House of Representatives joined in co-sponsoring this resolution, it has not yet been acted upon. The official Administration position was that the question of MIRV deployment would be a negotiable item at the Strategic Arms Limitation Talks (SALT) which first convened in Helsinki, Finland, in November of 1969, and resumed at Vienna in mid-April of 1970. I profoundly hope that the glacial-like progress toward mutual agreement on this and other issues will be accelerated.

The Bulletin of Atomic Scientists, a publication of nuclear physicists, carried on its initial cover a clock with the hands positioned at ten minutes to twelve. That was many years ago. The hands on the clock are still there, but doubtless they are closer to the hour. Despite some progress in negotiating a partial nuclear test ban treaty and a non-proliferation treaty, the basic issues of meaningful arms control remain to be resolved.

Unfortunately it seems to me that this is an area where the average self-satisfied Christian perceives neither duty nor obligation. He seems all too often blissfully and totally unaware of any linkage between his faith in God and the need to demonstrate any manifest concern that the world is rushing madly toward Armageddon. In the words of the World War Two song, he apparently would simply have us "Praise the Lord, and pass the ammunition." I am literally struck almost dumb — rare for a politician and hence the slight qualification — at the oblivious attitude toward the arms race held by many Christians. Some liberal churchmen are in the foreground of the battle, but most efforts by my evangelical friends are strictly rear echelon.

In this instance, it seems to me that we have completely inverted our theology. The theologian who believes as Harvey Cox, that the eighteenth century firmament of a transcendental God has collapsed around the ears of modern man, is not content to rely for his defense on planes, ships, and missiles armed with hydrogen warheads. He argues that man must seek an end to the arms race and develop other ways of maintaining a fragile peace between the super-powers, lest we end up like the characters in Nevil Shute's On the Beach, waiting for a poisonous radioactive cloud to envelop us.

Isaiah tells us that "the work of righteousness shall be peace" (Isaiah 32:17). Who shall furnish the righteousness that must lie at the very foundation of our effort to bring peace to a world weary of war and preparations for war, if it is not God's children? For it is not in our own righteousness, but clothed in God's righteousness, that our feet are shod with the preparation of the Gospel of peace. I would appeal to my Christian friends that, in the name of all humanity, we need to disenthrall ourselves and display some sense of urgency with respect to the issue of disarmament and arms control. Many will shrug this off as a matter impossible of resolution because of the treachery and intransigence of our Communist foe. I would reply to them in the words of Professor Shulman that it is not a matter of trust at all, but a matter involving the self-interest of every man, woman, and child on the face of the earth.

In a speech before the thirteenth meeting of the Canada-United States Interparliamentary Group in March, 1970, a Canadian Senator, M. Grattan O'Leary, said:

> Measured by human history, yours is a young country. Yet standing at the cockcrow and the morning star, you are at a pinnacle of power, with an awesome accountability to history. If in discharge of that responsibility you seek peace, then we as an ally and friend will walk with you always. But if peace be but a pause to identify the next enemy, if our world be unable to find a moral equivalent for the hydrogen bomb, then despair will have the last word, death's pale flag be again advanced, and this planet will cease to be the abode of men.

In a notable speech at the Air Force Academy in 1969, President Nixon spoke of the need to be willing to take "risks for peace." The moral leadership of the greatest nation in the world will be required if we are to make progress in this most difficult area. We used to hear of the missile gap, but it seems to me that the widest gap of all is the growing gap between our power to destroy the universe and our ability to adjudicate peacefully the disputes that arise between nations.

Richard Nixon spoke eloquently to this point in his 1969 Inaugural Address, when he held out the hope that somehow man in the remaining years of the twentieth century might turn away from the abyss of nuclear destruction and begin to explore the valley of opportunity represented by the peaceful uses of the atom:

> After a period of confrontation, we are entering an era of negotiation . . . . We cannot expect to make everyone our friend, but we can try to make no one our enemy. Those who would be our adversaries,

we invite to a peaceful competition — not in conquering territory or extending dominion but in enriching the life of men.

As a member since 1963 of the Joint Committee on Atomic Energy in the Congress, I have been profoundly impressed by the potential power for peace latent in the atom. When we consider the whole span of man's recorded history, it seems incredible to contemplate the possibilities that have opened up in the brief thirty-odd years since the German scientists Otto Hahn and Fritz Strassman literally stumbled on the principle of atomic fission in their search for one of the transuranium elements. Other great physicists like Niels Bohr and Albert Einstein had of course helped to lay the foundation for this discovery. But Hahn and Strassman's discovery that the uranium atom could be bombarded with neutrons and made to split, unleashing incredible amounts of energy, became one of the great building blocks of scientific progress. There followed swiftly the work of the great Italian-American scientist, Enrico Fermi, who conclusively demonstrated the feasibility of building a reactor and obtaining energy from the chain reaction that takes place when atomic fission occurs. Thus, a completely new source of energy was born, and the importance of that fact alone cannot be over-emphasized.

Dr. Glen Seaborg, Chairman of the Atomic Energy Commission, has said, "History reveals that the ascendency of states and civilizations was greatly affected by their control of energy . . . the way in which they used energy to extract and convert mineral resources." Just as the invention of the steam engine marked the beginning of the great Industrial Revolution, which so completely altered the primarily agrarian base of the world economy up through the eighteenth century, even so the discovery of this new source of energy has completely revolutionized our world of the twentieth century.

At the conclusion of World War Two, the newly-created Atomic Energy Commission, established in 1946 under the Atomic Energy Act, was still preoccupied with the military applications of atomic energy. In time, a thermonuclear weapon, the hydrogen bomb, was developed as a follow-up to the atomic bomb. However, it was ever the dream of the scientists who worked on the original Manhattan Project that the time would come, and the means would be found, to develop atomic energy for peaceful purposes. The passage by Congress in 1954 of the Amended Atomic Energy Act, and the promulgation by the Eisenhower Administration of its Atoms for Peace Program, meant that this great leap forward could begin. Since then, we have taken tremendous strides forward. The peaceful use of the atom is one of the great challenges of our age.

It has been estimated that the use of electrical energy in this country has doubled every ten years since the start of the present century. A distinguished scientist and former member of the A.E.C., Dr. Gerald Tape, estimates that by the year 2000, just thirty years from now, the total energy needs of the world will be three times as much as all the various forms of energy that have been utilized in the world since its very beginning. To meet these growing needs for energy, in the last dozen years or so the government has spent about $1.5 billion to develop civilian nuclear power, power generated in a plant not fueled by coal or oil or gas, but by an atomic reactor. It is estimated that by 1980 some twenty-five percent of all electric power will be from nuclear fuel. Today that estimate is undoubtedly far too low. Already there are twelve central station nuclear plants producing enough electricity to supply the needs of more than one million families. Another dozen or so new plants are under construction or in the planning stages. All this has happened in the last twenty years. It was on 20 December 1951, at the Argonne National Laboratory near Chicago, that for the first time in history enough electricity was produced by a nuclear reactor to light up four 200-watt bulbs.

Another peaceful application of atomic energy is seen in our space program. I was privileged to be at Vandenberg Air Force Base in California in the spring of 1965 when the United States successfully launched the first nuclear power reactor for space application. Mounted in a nose cone atop an Atlas-Agena rocket, this reactor was started up when it was about 700 miles out in space by a signal from a laboratory at Sunnyvale, California. It began to generate 500 watts of electricity and continued to operate successfully while whirling around in outer space for more than one month.

Today the atom is hard at work in the diagnosis and treatment of disease, in the handling and preservation of food, in fueling submarines, and in numerous construction and development projects under the Plowshare Program. This program, the name of which is derived from the prophecy of Isaiah, "They shall beat their swords into plowshares . . ." symbolizes the dilemma we face as we confront the two faces of the atom.

Atomic energy can be a force for evil or for good, depending upon the will of man. The same atomic energy that can provide useful electric power and other benefits to mankind could also account for 100 million casualties in the event of full-scale nuclear warfare. The very fact that today we must openly confront the possibility of a nuclear exchange with some enemy power points up the fact that, although we talk of such problems as the population explosion, famine, inflation, political instability, revolution, and the proliferation of nuclear weapons, man's biggest problem is still man himself.

This is the essence of the crisis of our atomic age. Our inability to discipline man's passions and his hatreds and greed has led to two great world wars and innumerable smaller ones in this century. We have not yet found the high road to the brotherhood of man. We must seek to perpetuate in our children not only a reverence for science and its accomplishments, but an awareness of its limitations; a deep and abiding faith in God and our religious heritage; a willingness to eschew the purely materialistic and consider also the spiritual aspect of man.

Before his death, our former Ambassador to the United Nations, Adlai Stevenson, observed that it had taken a revolution in science to produce the nuclear bomb, and to control it would require a revolution in politics. That revolution will not come about in a manner to bring peace to our world if it is led by those who in conspiratorial fashion have attempted to set up bomb factories in Manhattan. It will not bring peace in our time if it is led by those of either the radical left or the radical right. We need a spiritual revolution, led by men who have caught a vision of what this country should be and could be if our moral image in the world were to be illumined by a rekindled flame of righteousness.

I often visit the famed National Cathedral in Washington, one of the truly lovely churches in our land. Amid the solemn beauty of that great cathedral lies the crypt of Woodrow Wilson. It carries the following inscription written by the former President:

> The sum of the whole matter is this, that our civilization cannot survive materially unless it is redeemed spiritually. It can be saved only by becoming permeated with the Spirit of Christ, and being free and happy by the practices which spring out of that Spirit.

13
ONE
SOCIETY –
OPEN AND
EQUAL

One day during the summer of 1967 1 was attending a breakfast meeting at a leading hotel on exclusive Nob Hill in San Francisco. Several other Congressmen and I were discussing the problems of the Bay City with some local civic leaders, when four angry young blacks in the paramilitary outfits of the Black Panthers demanded admittance to our private dining room. They had heard that some Congressmen from Washington were there, and they had come to "tell it like it is."

One of their demands centered on the police. They wanted all regular city police barred from even entering the black section which was their turf. They would take over the policing of the area completely. Their demand was irrational in my judgment, along with many of the other demands which they included in the form of a Black Manifesto. But the real tragedy was the obvious lack of clear channels of communication between the black and white communities in that city. The young blacks showed distrust, fear, and even a deep suspicion that improvements suggested by sympathetic whites were actually only an opening wedge for a new form of exploitation. I had the feeling of two different societies headed for a violent collision.

Less than a year after this disturbing encounter in San Francisco, the Kerner Commission published its report on the causes of civil disorders in American cities. As I noted in Chapter One, I was particularly struck by the warning that our country was splitting into two societies, one black, one white — separate and unequal.

Though Negro Americans have made substantial gains in many areas, I believe that overall the divisions between black and white in this country are greater now than they were when the Kerner Report was published. White and black racism have fed on each other, and both have been nourished by a steady diet of ignorance, hate, prejudice, and fear.

Racism is in my view one of the most serious challenges facing American society today. It will be difficult to overcome, and we may not see an end to it for several generations, if at all. But if we do not begin to break down some of the walls now being built between white and black Americans, then I believe we will be courting a national tragedy as great or greater than the War between the States. We must not wait to act until we have passed the point of no return on the road from distrust to fear, from fear to hatred, from hatred to violence, and from violence to armed struggle.

I think many of us are beginning to realize how far along that road we have come already, and how perilously close we may be to the point of no return. There is a growing consensus among concerned, thoughtful Americans that we can no longer be content to talk equality while leaving the task to others. We must not fool ourselves. The task of opening up our society on an equal basis to black Americans will be formidable, despite the progress made in recent years. But we must begin. In this chapter I would like to discuss briefly four areas — jobs, housing, education, and the vote — in which the barriers must be broken down if we are ever going to have one society, open and equal.

A prime cause of despair in the slums and ghettos is the difficulty of finding a decent job. Negro men are three times as likely as whites to be in unskilled or service jobs. The concentration of male Negro employment at the lowest end of the occupational scale is the single most important source of poverty among Negroes.

Employment problems are a key contributor to family instability among blacks. In 1967 the proportion of non-white men divorced and separated was more than twice as high among the unemployed as among the employed. The number of non-white families headed by females is increasing, especially among the poor. In 1966 among non-white families earning less than $3,000 a year, forty-two percent had female heads.

The President's National Advisory Commission on Civil Disorders, in the Kerner Report, said: "With the father absent and the mother working, many ghetto children spend the bulk of their time on the streets — the streets of a crime-ridden, violence-prone, and poverty-stricken world." When they reach their teens, many stay on the streets. In the first nine months of 1967, the unemployment rate among non-white teen-agers was 26.7 percent. It was an age group well represented among the participants in civil disorders.

In 1967 the incidence of Negro poverty in the cities was three times that of whites. By then Negro family income in the cities had risen to a median of $5,623, but this was still only sixty-eight percent of white family income. A third of Negro families in the cities lived on $4,000 a year or less; sixteen percent of the whites lived on this level. More than two-thirds of Negro families in the cities lived on $8,000 a year or less, compared to less than half of the white families. Education did not reduce this disparity: blacks with eight years or less of school had incomes seventy-five percent that of whites with the same education; black college graduates had incomes seventy-four percent of their white counterparts.

A February, 1969, report of the U.S. Equal Employment Opportunity Commission concluded that the lower educational level of minority groups:

> . . . accounts for only about one-third of the differences in occupational ranking between Negro men and majority group men. The inevitable conclusion is that the other two-thirds must be attributed to discrimination, deliberate or inadvertent.

The report said job discrimination:

> . . . is strongest against Negro men in those industries which have a high proportion of Negro employees; have Negro and white employees; have Negro and white employees with average educational levels; have a high proportion of well-paying positions; or have a high proportion of their operations in the South . . . . In other words, it would seem that greater progress for Negroes brings forth progressively stronger discrimination against them.

Blacks own and operate less than one percent of the nearly five million private businesses in the country. Typically, these are small, marginal businesses: retail and service firms that cater to a constricted market. There are some twenty-odd, black-owned banks (out of a national total of more than 14,000, plus thirty-six black savings and loan associations and forty-three mortgage banks. There are about fifty black-owned life insurance companies, with combined assets of 0.2 percent of the industry's total, and only two that function nationally. There is a small, though growing number of black manufacturing firms. Still, fewer than three percent of the 1.5 million Americans who classify themselves as self-employed are black.

We need 140,000 new construction workers a year if we are to meet the housing goals of our country and provide a decent home and a suitable living environment for every American family. Yet, some of the old-line craft unions are tenaciously clinging to the idea that with artificial and rigid rules and restrictions they are going to keep blacks out of apprenticeship programs. They keep blacks from being journeymen in some of the highly-paid, highly-skilled crafts, which are the best opportunity for blacks to break out of the prison they now occupy in the ghettos.

The Nixon Administration, in the Philadelphia Plan, has encouraged communities to set hiring goals for minority workers in the construction trades, thus making a constructive start on the problem of job discrimination. But we must press ahead on all fronts, in all trades, and in the professions as well. The right to a job commensurate with his training and ability should not be denied to any American because of his color.

A second great obstacle to many black Americans is the lack of adequate, open housing. The Kerner Commission found that in every single city where racial violence had flared, dilapidated sub-standard housing was an element in the structure of discontent. In part the problem is due to the heavy out-migration by blacks from rural areas in the South. Just three decades ago, almost three-fourths of all Negroes in the United States lived in the South; when the last census was taken slightly more than half were still in the South. The 1970 census will almost certainly show that a majority now live in the North and West, and especially in the great urban centers. Today more than twelve million Negroes reside in central cities. It is conservatively estimated that in metropolitan areas like New York and Chicago, almost one out of four families live in housing that is substandard.

I remember asking the mayor of New York if something could be done to check the fantastic rate of in-migration into New York City, where in Harlem alone the population has more than tripled in less than a generation. His answer was that they come imbued with the vision of a better life than they knew in the sharecropper's shack in the Mississippi Delta; it would take armed guards in both the Lincoln and Holland Tunnels to keep them from pouring into Manhattan. And so poorly educated, disadvantaged blacks will continue to forsake the rural areas of the South and flock to our great urban centers. By 1985 it is estimated that their number will soar by seventy-two percent, so we will have 20.8 million blacks just in the central cities. This is a socio-economic fact of life which we can ignore only at our peril.

Unless conditions change to permit blacks to find decent housing in the suburbs and middle class urban neighborhoods, the ghetto population will grow by more than a third of a million each year. The inner cities, already powder kegs, could well erupt in violence even more bitter than the race riots of the sixties. It seems to me that the only way to defuse this situation, which is not only an affront to decency and morality but increasingly a question of preserving our internal peace and security, is to mount a two-pronged attack on discrimination in private housing and the quality and quantity of urban public housing.

It is for this reason that I have attached such great importance to open housing legislation, as we saw in Chapter One, and have been such a strong supporter of "Operation Breakthrough" and other programs developed by Housing and Urban Development Secretary George Romney. Operation Breakthrough is intended to develop new means of producing low-cost, mass-construction housing with the latest technologies and materials. Such programs are desperately needed if we are to overcome the present critical shortage of housing, let alone make some headway against the rot and decay now spreading in our great urban centers.

It is estimated that to meet our housing needs, we will have to have 2.6 million new units of housing per year for the next decade. We are building about half this number at the present time. Surely this is an area where our national priorities could be appropriately reordered, to begin to redeem the pledge our nation made twenty years ago, when Congress set a goal of "a decent home and suitable living environment for every American family."

A third critical area in the drive to open up our society is education. In many ways this is the most difficult and sensitive area of all, for our children are the most precious parts of our lives, and it is not easy to agree that they must bear part of the burden of integrating a society divided by their parents' fears. Yet if we are to accept the dispassionate conclusions of the Coleman Report on Equality of Educational Opportunity, commissioned by the President and Congress of the United States, we must admit that one of the key factors in the vicious cycle of black poverty, ignorance, apathy, and despair is separate and unequal schools. Dr. James Coleman, of Johns Hopkins University, and his associates found clear evidence that black children do appreciably better in integrated schools than in all-black ones, largely because they have stronger incentives to do better when exposed to middle-class white attitudes toward achievement and success. Slum children, whether in urban or rural areas, get little encouragement to excel in school in their home and family environment. If they are to develop their capacities fully, they must be exposed to the wider world beyond the slum and while they are young enough to have some chance of overcoming the apathy and indifference that haunt the streets of the Northern inner city and the byways of the rural South.

To fully confront the problem of segregated schools in the United States, we must be willing to deal with two kinds of segregation. One of these, *de jure* segregation, has been prevalent in the South as the result of Jim Crow laws intended to separate the races in all public situations. Bus depots and restaurants have proven easier to desegregate than schools, since discrimination in public commercial places is easier to identify and less deeply rooted in habit and custom. But a thorough legal foundation has now been laid for the effort to desegregate long-established dual school systems in the rural South, and I believe we must press on to finish this task. Then we may once again turn full attention to the quality of our children's education without worrying about its color.

But the real test of our nation's will to meet the challenge of racism and discrimination in education may well come not in the South, but in the North, where established housing patterns and neighborhood barriers have resulted in what we call *de facto* segregation, a matter of fact though not of law. It is said that the black ghetto in Chicago covers thirty square miles. Figures released by the Department of Health, Education and Welfare in the fall of 1969 indicated that public schools in Illinois were the most racially segregated in any state outside the deep South. Whereas on a nationwide basis 23.4 percent of black students attended predominantly white, desegregated public schools, in Illinois this figure was only 13.6 percent. In Chicago, only 3.2 percent of black students attended predominantly white schools.

If it is true, as the Coleman Report suggests, that integrated schooling is the greatest single identifiable factor in raising the motivation and achievement level of black school children, then I believe we have to try to make it available to them, by whatever means we can. This will not be a simple, painless problem to solve. It seems to me that basic to any solution must be an understanding of what our goals in American education really are. What are we trying to do in the neighborhood school? I would suggest that we are trying to do three things:

First, we want to protect and extend the quality of education our children are receiving. Not all of us are happy with present education programs: more than a few of our brightest students are bored; more than a few of our disadvantaged and slowest students are not getting the help that they should receive; more than a few parents are deeply concerned about the quality of education their children are getting.

The second thing we want to do is preserve the best characteristics of our neighborhood school systems. For many of us, the school is the centerpiece of our communities, the hub of the wheel, the symbol of a common concern for quality in our life together. We want to keep those elements which are essential to building community spirit and developing a better life in our neighborhoods.

Our third purpose is to build, across the nation, in the South and in the North, single public school systems in which any child, white or black, rich or poor, fast or slow, has the greatest possible opportunity for the best education he can get, without discrimination because of race, color, or creed. This purpose grows out of a traditional American concern for equal treatment of all citizens. It was made the law of the land in the 1954 Brown decision, which rendered invalid the "separate but equal" approach to education.

Most Americans would agree on these goals, I think. Our difficulty comes in trying to implement them. I for one see no easy answer that we can expect to work in every case. In some cases the answer may involve busing. I know that controversy swirls around the word, and emotions run high at the sound of it. To some the familiar yellow bus has become a hated symbol of ruthless and impersonal government by fiat, government by court decree, without any understanding of local conditions and human problems. To some it is synonymous with declining standards of education, disciplinary problems in the classrooms, and pervasive fear in the halls.

But we have to put busing in perspective. In testimony before the Rules Committee in February of 1970, Secretary of Health, Education and Welfare Robert Finch indicated that busing must be considered as only one potential alternative in the whole complicated equation of trying to bring both quality and desegregated education to the American school system. Given the limited material resources of a particular district, busing may not necessarily be the best way to achieve this goal. It may well be true, to cite a specific case, that a $180 million expenditure to bus children across sprawling Los Angeles is not the best means of raising the level of educational achievement and affording each child an equal right to quality schooling regardless of race or color or creed in that system.

We cannot be sidetracked by the issue of busing. As a nation and as individual communities we have to come back to the central question: how best to provide, with a minimum of anguish and unrest, desegregated quality education for all our children. Our goal must be to give every American child — black or white, rich or poor, slow or swift — the opportunity to develop his talents to the fullest extent possible. The experience of a free and open society must begin in childhood.

Our local communities have a vitally important role to play in the solution of this problem. Busing may not necessarily be the best way. If not, then we must find a better way — more decent, more realistic, less expensive, more far-sighted. Let us together find the way that will work for ourselves and our neighbors, white and black.

I believe Christians may have a particularly important role to play within our local communities. This may be a case in which a spirit of genuine Christian love could prove that our system can indeed be made to work. Without examining the merits of the controversy over the yellow school bus, it is still possible to conclude that if our Christian love is broad enough to extend to our neighbor's child, we will be willing to support those actions that will assure him equal educational opportunity. But first we must be willing to look at the problem with a Christian conscience, and in a spirit that says, "I will judge this issue with a heart that is ruled, not by prejudice or hatred, but by the same love that Christ showed toward me."

A final area of vital importance in the effort to open and integrate our society is the right of every citizen to vote. Many of us take the ballot so much for granted that we do not even exercise our right to use it. We forget that for decades and even centuries in this country, many Americans were denied that right because their color was black.

Since the Congress passed the historic Voting Rights Act of 1965, banning discriminatory literacy tests and other forms of political coercion in states where such devices had been used to bar Negroes from the polls, more than one million blacks have been enfranchised and added to the electoral rolls. In the first session of the 91st Congress there was an unsuccessful effort, supported by the Administration, to dilute the Act by extending its enforcement provisions to states which did not have these problems.

I opposed the dilution of the 1965 Act, and in so doing broke with many of my respected colleagues and close friends. I did so because I believed that to weaken this law would be a symbolic retreat in the effort to make our society one, open and equal. I felt that we simply could not afford to go backward in this important effort, at the very time when we are trying to prove that our system does work, that it will respond to the clear needs of all our citizens.

Two things must be done to preserve the fabric of our society, I believe. First, we must improve life in the ghettos and give a vital ray of hope to those who live there. Secondly, we must integrate substantial numbers of blacks into society outside the ghettos. In my judgment this is the only way to defuse the racial tensions that may otherwise tear our society apart.

What can we do in our local communities? We should, for one, encourage our local governments to pass open occupancy housing ordinances. On the federal level I have supported legislation like this which would apply in states and communities that do not adopt their own.

We can also encourage an accelerated effort to open up occupational opportunities heretofore barred to blacks. If this does not occur, we will have to resign ourselves to the notion that the federal government must be the employer of last resort.

Significant changes in personal attitudes are absolutely essential if we are to encourage responsible blacks to disavow the pronouncements and acts of the apostles of hatred. Whitney Young, a responsible black leader, has said: "There are no longer militants and moderates in the Negro leadership. There are the sane and the insane, the builders and the burners, those within and those without society." We must be willing to extend the hand of help and reconciliation if we would strengthen the hand of those who would build, not burn.

Christians once again have a special responsibility to lead in this effort. It is tragic but true that many of us are as guilty of the sin of racism as the most hardened unbelievers. Do we believe that all men are creatures of one blood? Do we accept the divine injunction of our Lord, that the second great commandment is "love thy neighbor as thyself"? Or do we in the next breath pray, "But Lord, let not my neighbor be black"? We sing that "Jesus loves the little children . . . red and yellow, black and white." But do we somehow feel differently about the children once they have grown up?

We give generously to missionaries so they can take the Gospel to black Africa. But that is not the limit of our responsibility. We have to minister to the Afro-American in our midst. We cannot thrust that responsibility to the outer, remote circumference of our own personal experience. We cannot tell the missionary to go out and love the black man, the yellow man, the brown man of Africa and Asia, and then refuse ourselves to be put down next to our black neighbor and show the same love.

We must begin to think of discrimination in terms of one man, one woman, one child, one job. We must take everything we read and apply it to one human being. We must find that one. We must search him out, even though we may not like what we find.

Christian laymen need to cement closer ties with black churches, so that a cooperative program of Christian witness can be effectively implemented to bring the message of Christ's love to the under-churched, or perhaps totally unchurched, in areas that exist in almost every city of any size. Christian businessmen should take the lead in instituting nondiscriminatory programs of basic education and training so that blacks will be able to qualify for better paying jobs. Christian politicians should make every effort to bring blacks more fully into the political process in their local communities. On every front, we must be willing to lay our faith on the line in the battle to make of our America one society, open and equal.

All men are created in God's image. Racial bigotry is thus an affront to the God of creation Himself. It is for Christians to blaze the trail to racial understanding and racial justice, for we can only hope to bridge the awful gap that has opened between black and white in our society with the instrumentality of Christian love.

14
POVERTY
AMID
PLENTY

Mayor John Lindsay of New York, Vice Chairman of the Kerner Commission appointed by President Johnson to study the causes of the riots that swept American cities in the summers of the mid-Sixties, has observed that "America's affluence is as close as the television set to the poor, yet it is as remote as 100 years of prejudice." Doubtless one of the reasons that affluent Americans have been so oblivious to the poverty in our midst is that unlike the rich, the poor seldom find their way onto television. They have been a hidden minority, one of which we were largely unaware until the publication in the early Sixties of such books as Michael Harrington's *The Other America.*

I went looking for poverty one summer day several years ago. The Ford Foundation was sponsoring a series of walking tours for Congressmen from rural or suburban areas, to give them a glimpse of the other America. I joined the group on several occasions, and it proved to be an eye-opening experience. We visited such places as Harlem, Hunter's Point in San Francisco, West Oakland, the Watts area of Los Angeles, and the Hough ghetto in Cleveland. For periods of two or three days at a time, members of Congress walked city streets, visited homes, and saw conditions we would not have believed could exist in our country.

The sidewalks of New York, subject of some of yesteryear's most joyous lyrics, were not a particularly pleasant sight that day — not in Harlem, not even in parts of Manhattan, Brooklyn, and the Bronx. The courtyards of ghetto tenements were piled high with rubbish — the playgrounds were breeding grounds and eating grounds for rats the size of cats. I remember stepping across the rotting sill of a doorway into a typical slum tenement and talking to a sad-eyed little man with no fingers on one hand. They had been lost in an industrial accident. He was unemployed, his compensation exhausted, his wife pregnant, and six indescribably dirty little urchins huddled behind her skirts. I have never looked into the eyes of any man who seemed so utterly bleak and barren of hope. He was only one of many hundreds of thousands. Perhaps even with his handicap he could some day find a job which would enable him to support his family, but first he would have to learn English. He was a Puerto Rican who had left the hovels of a slum in San Juan to find a better life in the United States.

In 1964 our nation mounted a campaign against the newly-discovered poverty in our midst. Directed from the Office of Economic Opportunity, the war on poverty was launched in a burst of fanfare and faddism. Everyone was against poverty, and for a time it seemed that we might marshal the will and the means to alleviate some of the sorest blights in our urban and rural slums.

Sometime after the mid-Sixties, the will began to die and the means began to disappear, claimed by other priorities like the war in Vietnam. Today I think we recognize that this problem, like the problem of racism and the problem of war, admits of no easy solution. In many areas of our country, particularly the hard-core urban slums, poverty seems inseparably tied to race. In other areas, notably Appalachia and the rural South, poverty knows no color. In all these areas it is characterized by the interlocking tentacles of underemployment, hunger and malnutrition, ignorance, ill health, apathy and despair, lack of legal redress against exploitation by landowners and landlords, and the lack of any family planning to keep from bringing more poor children into the world.

We discussed problems of employment and education in the last chapter, because they are more closely associated with racial problems. In this chapter I would like to focus briefly on the problems of hunger and malnutrition, and the need for family planning services among the poor.

We may argue over the definitions of such terms as hunger and malnutrition, and the extent to which these conditions are prevalent in America, but the fact remains that they are real and serious problems. As President Nixon put it in a message to Congress: "That hunger and malnutrition should persist in a land such as ours is embarrassing and intolerable." He went on to say that more is at stake than the welfare of some sixteen million Americans who need food assistance. In his words, "Something very like the honor of American democracy is at issue."

Some people seem to think that because there is not widespread famine or mass starvation, there is no hunger in America. Hunger in the United States does not have the visibility that it has had in Biafra or India. As testimony before Senator George McGovern's Select Committee on Nutrition and Human Needs has disclosed, in America it assumes more subtle forms, such as increasing the rate of infant mortality and making hungry children and adults more vulnerable to sickness and less able to work.

In 1968 some 76,000 American babies died during infancy. That means that for every thousand live births, there were about twenty-two deaths. It may come as a shock to some that the United States trails twelve other nations in this regard. In poor rural and urban areas, infant mortality is at least two to three times higher than in our more favored communities, with infant deaths running between fifty and one hundred for every thousand live births. In addition, the prematurity rate is from two to four times higher in poor communities than it is in middle-class areas. The maternal mortality rate is at least twice as high among the poor as among the middle class.

While these facts cannot be ascribed to a single variable, they can be traced at least indirectly to malnutrition in poorer communities. Most infant deaths occur when the child is underweight. There is a direct correlation between the size of the child and the nutritional deficiencies of both the mother and the child. Severe nutritional deprivation during the first eighteen months of life can also cause permanent and irreversible brain damage.

It appears that the greatest damage resulting from inadequate nutrition occurs during gestation, infancy, and certainly during the years prior to formal schooling. For this reason most discussion about hunger and malnutrition tends to concentrate on the potential mental and physical injuries to infants and children, and the need for improved nutritional services for pregnant women and young children.

In addition to this, however, serious cases of hunger and malnutrition prevail among all age groups in our poorer communities. Teachers have reported many cases of children who should be coming to school hungry to learn, yet are too hungry to learn and in such pain that they are either sent home or taken to the school nurse. Hunger is also a problem among our poorer senior citizens who live alone and subsist mainly on liquid foods that provide inadequate sustenance.

What is the government doing about hunger and malnutrition? In 1935 Congress authorized the Secretary of Agriculture to use a portion of U.S. Customs receipts to buy farm goods and give them to welfare institutions. Over the years these food programs have been expanded. In 1946 the Congress established what is known as the commodity distribution program, which makes available to the poor at no cost some twenty-two commodities acquired by the government as surplus foods under price support laws.

The other type of food program sponsored by the federal government is the food stamp program, which became permanent in 1964 under the Food Stamp Act. This program was designed to increase the food-buying power of low income families through a government subsidy. For a small amount of money, poor families may purchase stamps worth a larger amount, which may be redeemed for food at local food stores. Families with low incomes may purchase these stamps for fifty cents per member, and large families pay a total low rate of $3.00.

It is estimated that a total of 6.7 million Americans are being served by one of these two programs, with 3.1 million receiving food stamps and another 3.6 million receiving commodities. A county cannot take advantage of both programs; it must choose either the food stamps or the commodities.

The fact that nearly seven million Americans are now being served by these programs is misleading in several respects. First, there is some evidence that these programs are not reaching those most in need of them. If we assume, as does the President, that there are some sixteen million Americans in need of food assistance, then it is obvious that we are reaching less than half that many needy persons.

Second, there is evidence that the present service to those who receive these benefits is woefully inadequate. Witness after witness testifying before the Senate Select Committee on Hunger said the needy have to travel miles to purchase food stamps, they have to wait in line for hours to be certified, eligibility requirements are unrealistic, and welfare officials are unsympathetic to their needs.

Recent field trips by the Senate Select Committee on Nutrition and Human Needs have served to give greater visibility to the problem of hunger in America and to the demands for a complete overhaul of federal food programs. At the same time, the Nixon Administration has been studying the problem and preparing a program to meet the needs of underfed, malnourished Americans.

In his message to Congress in May of 1969, the President recognized that the problem does not lend itself to fast and easy solutions. He noted an apparent need to revise drastically the current programs, so that they will be better suited to meet the needs of the poor. There is need both for more food assistance money and a greater educational effort as to the right foods and proper diet.

The President also asked the Secretary of Agriculture to see that food assistance is expanded to some 400 counties that are not participating in either of the two food programs. To eliminate some of the main difficulties of the past in the food stamp program, the president asked that more stamp distribution points be established, that there be prompter and simpler certification of recipients, that financing arrangements be made available, and that the possibility of mailing food stamps be explored.

In addition, the national nutritional survey of the Public Health Service is being expanded to provide more adequate statistical information on the extent of hunger and malnutrition, and more research on the relation between mental retardation and malnutrition will be conducted. A greater role is also envisioned for medical schools in working on these problems.

While the immediate goal is to eliminate hard-core hunger, and to assist those unable to provide for their total food needs, it is most important to look beyond the issue of hunger and view it in the total context of poverty in America. We should not consider the current food programs as permanent operations; they are stop-gap measures until we can complete a comprehensive overhaul of the entire public assistance program which President Nixon has initiated as we saw in Chapter Ten. None of our citizens relish the prospect of spending their entire lives in bread lines. Instead, we must think in terms of making the welfare system one in which there are proper incentives for getting off the welfare rolls and onto the work rolls. We must think in terms of elevating the nation's poor above the poverty levels and connecting them with the productive economy. The present programs have been roundly criticized by welfare recipients and taxpayers alike, and with justification. Instead of moving the nation toward a decent and productive life for all, they have only tended to institutionalize poverty and make the lot of our poor more hopeless and helpless. The President's Family Assistance Plan, providing for a $1,600 income floor for a family of four and new incentives to train and find work, will go a long way toward reversing this trend.

There are other problems we must take into account in connection with hunger in America. One of them is family planning. A statistic that greatly alarms me is the fact that every year there are about 450,000 unwanted births among the poor and near poor in America. It is little wonder that many mothers and children suffer from malnutrition when you consider the fact that these families are not financially prepared to have more children. One in five American families report that their last child was unwanted. Out of five million low income women who would probably use family planning services, only one in five now receives such help.

In my Congressional district there are nearly 9,000 poverty level women between the ages of eighteen and forty-four, and yet not one of the seven counties provides any means other than the private physician for family planning services. Only a few poverty level women can afford the services of a private physician. If we apply the national statistics on unwanted children to my district, it would mean that in 1968 there were 1,500 unwanted children born in this district of seven counties. I do not suggest that none of these children will be properly cared for, but I wonder how many of them will suffer permanent mental or physical retardation or suffer from malnutrition as a result of the family's financial situation. How many of these births could have been prevented if low cost family planning services had been available? Although five of the seven counties have Community Action agencies, not one of them has an OEO neighborhood health center, and not one of them has a U.S. Public Health Service facility.

The demand for adequate food and family planning services must emanate from neighborhood groups. These groups should have a role in the administration of such programs. This is not something that can be forced on the people by the federal government or anyone else. Even considering the increases in the federal budget for food and poverty programs, it is clear that to be effectively used this money must be channeled into programs that are close to the people. The government does not have unlimited resources or answers. More answers must be sought at the state and local levels, and in the private and independent sectors, if we are ever to achieve our objectives. Communities are beginning to wake up to the fact that involvement begins with an "I."

I remember seeing two adjoining newspaper stories in one of our large metropolitan dailies which brought home to me the agonizing contrast between the affluent and the other America. One article was about a dramatic increase in the automobile accident rate in one of the city's affluent suburbs. The rate had gone up sharply because the teenage sons and daughters of wealthy parents all had their own cars. The adjoining column described conditions in a county barely twenty-five miles away from the affluent suburb. There was a picture of a father ill with tuberculosis, together with his wife and seven children. For budgetary reasons the state had been obliged to reduce welfare payments. As a result this family was faced with a financial crisis so severe that they did not know where to go for help.

Poverty and hunger are not problems that we can shun if we would truly serve our Lord and our fellow-man. In Matthew 25, Christ makes our responsibility very clear when He foretells the day that the Son of Man will come in His glory, to sit in judgment upon the righteous and the damned:

> Then shall he say also unto them on the left hand, Depart from me, ye cursed, into everlasting fire, prepared for the devil and his angels:
> For I was an hungered, and ye gave me no meat: I was thirsty, and ye gave me no drink:
> I was a stranger, and ye took me not in: naked, and ye clothed me not: sick, and in prison, and ye visited me not.
> Then shall they also answer him, saying, Lord, when saw we thee an hungered, or athirst, or a stranger, or naked, or sick, or in prison, and did not minister unto thee?
> Then shall he answer them, saying, Verily I say unto you, Inasmuch as ye did it not to one of the least of these, ye did it not to me.

15
CRIME,
VIOLENCE
AND
THE LAW

The most telling domestic theme of Richard Nixon's 1968 campaign for the Presidency was the crisis of law and order in America and the need for a nation-wide war on crime. Some liberal commentators and candidates tried to blunt the edge of the issue, charging that "law 'n' order" had become code words for racism. Perhaps a more polished phrase would have been "domestic tranquility," but it was arrant nonsense to ask that Americans suddenly stop talking about a critical problem because it might be a disguised way of expressing racial prejudice.

The American people were not so easily fooled. In eight years during the 1960's serious crime in the United States had risen six times as fast as the population. The man who had been robbed, the woman who had been assaulted, the family whose home had been burglarized — these people were hardly being racist when they cited their experiences as proof that there had been a breakdown of law and order. Law and order was and is a legitimate issue, for notwithstanding the first year's efforts of an Administration trying to begin a new war with old weapons, the dimensions of the crime problem in America are as grave in 1970 as they were in 1968.

Serious crime in the United States, as registered in Federal Bureau of Investigation Crime Index figures, rose eleven percent in 1969. Among violent crimes, forcible rape increased sixteen percent, robbery thirteen percent, and murder seven percent. The increase in total crime, including crimes against property, was greatest not in large urban centers (up nine percent), but in the suburbs (up thirteen percent) to which so many middle-class Americans have fled to get away from such things as crime.

In themselves these figures may not seem overly impressive. It is difficult to imbue statistics with the fascination of money, flesh, and blood; yet I would guess that few readers of these pages have been entirely immune from the growing fear that haunts not just our city streets but increasingly our suburban neighborhoods and country roads. The alarming rise in crimes of violence, unless it is checked, could turn our citizens into fearful strangers suspicious of each other, and make of our nation the very kind of closed and repressive society which our Founding Fathers were so determined to prevent.

A tragic symbol of this possibility is our nation's capital, which in recent years has had one of the fastest growing crime rates in the United States. In 1969 alone, total offenses climbed twenty-seven percent in the District of Columbia, to 62,000 incidents of serious crime. Washington has one of the highest rates of increase in violent crime, including murder, of any city in the nation. Armed robbery increased forty-four percent in the District in 1969; one of these statistics was a member of my own staff.

Newspaper headlines have chronicled the dramatic increases cited above. Breakfast talk often centers on a particularly gory assault of the previous evening. Washington, the beautiful federal capital on the Potomac, is in danger of becoming a fear-ridden city. In his 1970 State of the Union Message, President Nixon challenged those Senators and Congressmen who live close to the Capitol to leave their cars in the Capitol garage and walk home that night. So far as I know, not one of them took him up on it.

One of the most disturbing trends of all in recent years has been the rise in juvenile crime. In the words of a Congressional Quarterly Report on Crime and Justice, "To talk about crime in America is to talk about kids." The Commission on Law Enforcement and Administration of Justice, appointed by President Lyndon Johnson, found that fifteen-year-olds have a higher arrest rate than any other age group in our society. The Kerner Commission found that fifteen to twenty-four-year-olds are more highly represented in civil disorders and riots than any other age group. The Select Committee on Crime in the House of Representatives found that juvenile arrests for narcotics offenses had climbed 800 percent in the past decade, while federal spending for control of juvenile crime actually decreased. If children are the most precious assets a society has, then it would make sense for our society to begin to take this problem seriously.

During the decade of the Sixties another kind of crime cast a lengthening shadow over American life. Some called it the Mafia; others, the Mob, the Black Hand, the Syndicate, the Cosa Nostra, or simply organized crime. In the early part of the decade many Americans were not even aware of its existence, and former member Joe Valachi could say of it, "Nobody will listen. Nobody will believe . . . . This Cosa

Nostra, it's like a second government. It's too big." Now the Mob is romanticized in popular fiction like *The Godfather*, Mario Puzo's best selling novel, and *Time* Magazine estimates that the annual profits of organized crime are greater than those of U.S. Steel, AT&T, General Motors, Standard Oil of New Jersey, General Electric, Ford, IBM, Chrysler, and RCA combined — making it easily the largest business enterprise in the world.

We now know that the hard core of the enterprise is La Cosa Nostra, which consists of some 5,000 members organized since the 1930's into "families" in major cities across the nation, but especially east of the Mississippi. The Mob has ties with virtually every form of crime known in the United States, but its particular specialties have been the infiltration and take-over of legitimate business, the undermining and corruption of government officials and labor leaders, and the exploitation of vice, from gambling and prostitution to a near monopoly on large-scale traffic in narcotics.

It is estimated that the Mob may be involved in running up to 5,000 business concerns, with profits in billions of dollars. Florida Attorney General Earl Faircloth, in hearings before the House Select Committee on Crime, said our failure to identify organized crime as substantive crime is at least partly due to the use of old police methods. He pointed out that whereas most crimes involve a single, plainly visible incident in a particular place, and a culprit who is either found and prosecuted or escapes, "organized crime has none of these components . . . . The perpetrator is unavailable, the act is continuous and widespread, and the event, while visible, is concealed by its apparent legality." Faircloth suggests that we badly need more law officers trained to deal with the methods of organized crime.

The infiltration of government by the Mafia is even more insidious in its ramifications, for here the law is not merely unenforced but mocked. In 1969 the Justice Department began a crackdown on blatant corruption in Newark and other Northeastern municipal governments. But the problem is not confined either to the Northeast or to local government. Ralph Salerno, former New York police officer and one of the leading experts on the Mob, estimates that Mafia pressure might influence the votes of as many as twenty-five Members of Congress. Salerno says, "Organized crime will put a man in the White House some day and he won't know it until they hand him the bill."

Narcotics, over which the Mafia has a virtual monopoly, may be more responsible for the burgeoning crime rate than any other single factor. Once a junkie is hooked on heroin or any other hard drug, he can be made to do almost anything to get his regular fix.

The actual cost of crime is rarely measured. Research done by the House Republican Conference, using figures from the President's Crime Commission Report, showed that in the Sixties crime took out of the economy as much as four times the amount spent by all levels of government to combat it. The average annual cost of crime was about twenty-one billion dollars, while total government spending on police, prisons, courts, and counsel annually ran to just over four billion.

But the real tragedy of the spread of crime in America cannot be told in terms of dollars. It must be told in human terms: lives ruined or lost, careers destroyed, hopes turned awry, families broken. Much of the toll we pay annually in "human resources" is directly attributable to crime.

What can we do to fight this growing scourge? The first thing is that we must understand as clearly as possible the causes of crime and move to combat them at the source. Crime is not a simple phenomenon. As the President's Commission on Law Enforcement and the Administration of Justice put it:

> A skid row drunk lying in a gutter is crime. So is the killing of an unfaithful wife. A Cosa Nostra conspiracy to bribe public officials is crime. So is a strong-arm robbery by a 15-year-old boy. The embezzlement of a corporation's funds by an executive is crime. So is the possession of marijuana cigarettes by a student. These crimes can no more be lumped together for purposes of analysis than can measles and schizophrenia, or lung cancer and a broken ankle. As with disease, so with crime: if causes are to be understood, if risks are to be evaluated, and if preventive or remedial actions are to be taken, each kind must be looked at separately. Thinking of "crime" as a whole is futile.

Thus we must be intelligent in approaching the causes of crime. Where it is likely that anti-social behavior can be deterred by checking the first impulses of a potential criminal through stronger penalties and more police, let us have them. Where we are faced with the psychopathology of a hardened criminal who will not be deterred, or the young first offender who might yet be reclaimed for a normal productive life, let us focus on the quality of our prisons and our methods of rehabilitation.

The National Commission on the Causes and Prevention of Violence, chaired by Dr. Milton Eisenhower, emphasized in its final report in late 1969 that crime often reflects the inadequacies of our society — poverty, poor housing, lack of decent jobs, inferior schooling — especially as these inadequacies reinforce each other in our great urban slums:

> It is the ghetto slum that is disproportionately responsible for violent crime, by far the most acute aspect of the problem of violence in the United States today.
>
> To be a young, poor male; to be undereducated and without means of escape from an oppressive urban environment; to want what the society claims is available (but mostly to others); to see around oneself illegitimate and often violent methods being used to achieve material gain; and to observe others using these means with impunity — all this is to be burdened with an enormous set of influences that pull many toward crime and delinquency. To be also a Negro, Puerto Rican or Mexican-American and subject to discrimination and segregation adds considerably to the pull of these criminogenic forces.
>
> Safety in our cities requires nothing less than progress in reconstructing urban life . . . .

The fact that severe social inadequacies have greatly contributed to the present crisis of law and order should give us greater incentive, if any is yet needed, to readjust our national priorities and directly confront these inadequacies.

But the Eisenhower Commission also spotlighted a second major concern, which I think more and more thoughtful Americans are coming to share. Much of the crime in this country can be traced, directly and indirectly, to a climate of violence unparalleled in the "civilized" world. The Commission found that:

> The United States is the clear leader among modern, stable democratic nations in its rates of homicide, assault, rape and robbery, and it is at least among the highest in incidence of group violence and assassination.

Among the most important contributing elements to this climate of violence are the glorification of violence in American and particularly frontier history, the heavy emphasis on violence in the mass media, and the relative availability of firearms in every part of the United States.

We cannot do much to change our history, and if we are honest with ourselves we have to admit that our nation was conceived in the violence of revolution and grew in large measure in times of war, first against the French and Indians, then against the British, then against the Mexicans, the Plains Indians, the Filipinos, and the collective enemies of two world wars, But it is one thing to be honest and dispassionate about the violence that plays such a large part in our history, and another to glorify it. When Rap Brown says that "violence is as American as cherry pie," he implies that it is not only an accepted but a valued part of American life. I submit that violence can only be valued in a very sick society, and I fervently hope that as a nation we will never come even to accept violence, let alone value it.

The mass media have had a tremendous impact in legitimatizing violence, and particularly in giving children the impression that violence is a normal part of life in our society. Psychiatrist Fredric Wertham, a noted authority on violence, points out that whereas the Leopold-Loeb case caused a sensation thirty years ago because the accused murderers were only eighteen, today "it is not uncommon to see deliberate murder committed by children of twelve or thirteen or even younger. Children of eight or nine are found torturing one another or commiting serious acts of sadism." Not long ago the nation's capital was shocked when a fourteen-year-old girl named "Muffin" was arrested with two friends in the brutal crowbar slaying of her affluent father. Our children have been conditioned to accept violence as normal, and our society is beginning to reap the awful fruits — on the campus, in the streets, even in our schools.

Americans have debated for years whether the availability of firearms has caused the increase in violence in our society, or contributed to it, or merely reflected it. The Eisenhower Commission, noting that most owners of firearms use them responsibly and that guns generally facilitate rather than cause violence, nevertheless found that "the availability of guns contributes substantially to violence in American society." There are now some 90 million firearms in the United States, practically one for every two Americans. Half of the nation's sixty million households possess at least one gun. Surely it is time for this nation to take concrete steps to control the illegitimate use of firearms without interfering with the rights of hunters, collectors, and competition shooters to use their guns responsibly. A restrictive licensing system for handguns — which are most often used in violent crimes and seldom used in sport — has been strongly recommended by the Commission on

Violence, and would be a significant first step toward curbing the illegitimate use of firearms.

These and other measures can be taken to try to reduce the climate of violence and crime that seems to grow stronger year by year in America, but in the end we are left with the concrete problem of dealing with crime and violence themselves — specific anti-social acts increasing at such a rapid rate that they threaten not only our property and peace of mind but the fabric of social order itself, and indeed our very lives.

It will be no easy task to bring crime in America under control, but to begin intelligently we need to understand what role each level of government can be expected to play. The tradition of law enforcement in America has always been a local one. Our communities have been jealous of their right to maintain order, and we have been more than a little suspicious of the kind of national police force which in other countries has often become the repressive arm of a tyrannical autocracy. Yet the federal government has a clear and important responsibility to control crime that crosses state lines. A strong federal effort is needed particularly in such areas as crime in interstate commerce, white collar and organized crime, narcotics, pornography, and crime in the nation's capital.

The Nixon Administration has taken strong intiatives in each of these areas. In his 1970 State of the Union Message, the President stated that the executive branch had done everything it could under existing laws, but that new weapons were needed. Administration proposals dealing with street crime, organized crime, narcotics, pornography, and crime in the District of Columbia have been pigeonholed for months in Congressional committees controlled by Democrats. Only public pressure will force action on these important bills.

Beyond his concern for fulfilling the federal role in law enforcement, President Nixon has recognized that the crisis of crime and violence is deep enough in our land that local law enforcement agencies will need all the help they can get. "If there is one area where the word 'war' is appropriate," he said, "it is in the fight against crime." Accordingly, the President announced that while he had ordered stringent cuts in the budgets of most executive departments, he was requesting a doubling of federal aid to local law enforcement agencies. In practical terms, this meant that the federal budget for the war on crime would be increased by 310 million dollars, to 1.3 billion in fiscal 1971, as compared with 2 billion for the war on poverty.

It is local law enforcement agencies, the police departments of our cities and towns, that must wage the central campaign in the war against crime. In recent years no professional group in our society has stirred as much controversy and vilification as the men in blue, yet no other group is so vital in the attempt to preserve the fabric of our social order and make American streets safe once again. Policemen are human beings. The cop on the beat offers a convenient target for hatreds and resentments that have nothing to do with him personally. He is called upon to bear tremendous pressure without breaking discipline or losing his head. It is a tribute to the strength and leadership of our police profession that in the turbulence of the Sixties the great majority of American policemen did their jobs with quiet courage in the face of mounting abuse.

Local police departments must have the support of their communities if they are to do their job. Along this two-way street, police must respect the private rights of citizens and community leaders must appreciate the responsibilities of the man on the beat. Both have a stake in maintaining order and communication. The most effective means of reducing crime developed in recent years — such as taking policemen out of squad cars and putting them on walking beats in two-man teams, or putting unemployed teen-agers into squad cars to help make rounds and develop personal relationships with policemen — have involved strengthening the ties of individual police to the communities they serve.

But our police also need to be strengthened in numbers, pay, equipment, and training. They are among the lowest paid professions; they have not been given the equipment available to crime control through modern technology; and their numbers are too small to discharge their responsibilities effectively. Above all, they need continual training in the art of working with community leaders, to strengthen that fragile fabric of social order which is the clearest indicator of community health and strength. These are priorities which desperately need to be met. They cannot be put off if we are to reclaim our cities and towns.

At the same time, we must remember that the coin of justice has two sides, one of order, the other of freedom. Theodore White, in *The Making of the President, 1968* says:

> American history begins with a contradiction, and this heritage, in 1968, was to haunt us. In its chartering document, the Constitution, two high and conflicting purposes were set out for the American government. In its preamble, the document told Americans that we, the people,

establish this Constitution "in order to form a more perfect union, establish justice, insure domestic tranquility, provide for the common defense." But then it went on, adding as an afterthought, and under pressure, a Bill of Rights guaranteeing the undefined rights of assembly, petition, freedom of speech, press and thought. And thus, by derivation, the right of demonstration and confrontation. In 1968 the first guarantee, of domestic tranquility, was to be challenged by the later guarantee, of assembly and confrontation — and no one could say which had priority over the other.*

The answer was that neither could be given priority. If justice is to prevail, then neither freedom nor order can be allowed to take precedence over the other. Tensions between the two must be reconciled by the process of law, whose function it is to preserve individual freedom to the broadest extent possible within a framework of social order.

White was writing with reference to the student demonstrations of 1968 and the specter of violence which loomed in that election year. But the same tension exists with respect to crime, for we will destroy both the majesty of the law and justice itself if, in our haste to restore order, we debase those individual rights which are the only guarantees of a free society — including not just the freedoms White mentioned, but the others guaranteed in the Bill of Rights: freedom against unreasonable search and seizure, freedom against self-incrimination, the right to a speedy public trial by jury, the right to bear arms, freedom of religion, and the rest.

It has been said that respect for the law is the religion of liberty. Never in our history has the law faced such a test of its ability to reconcile the conflicting demands of freedom and order. To successfully meet that test will require the full support of a citizenry deeply committed to the most basic principles of American democracy. We have not seen the end of crime and violence, for we live in times marked by conflict, turbulence, and fear. But with God's help, and with faith in the principles that have brought us safely through other storms, the rising tides of crime and violence can be checked and the religion of liberty prevail.

---

* Theodore H. White, *The Making of a President, 1968* (Atheneum Publishers, 1969), p. 221.

16
THE
FACE
OF THE
EARTH

Early in 1970 an arresting photograph of New York Harbor appeared in several of our leading magazines. It showed two great monuments to the American spirit. In the background was the Statue of Liberty, symbol of freedom and opportunity to the desolate immigrants who sought refuge on America's shores. In the foreground was a mountain of garbage, the wretched refuse of those teeming shores, being towed by barge to a dumping ground at sea.

The photograph highlighted a paradox that has come to haunt us with startling suddenness at the outset of a new decade. There is no question that the United States is the richest, most productive nation in the world. We have become accustomed to measuring ourselves in terms of what we produce — how many we have of such-and-such, how big they are, and what the rate of increase in their production will be. All during the Sixties, despite a frustrating war abroad and growing unrest at home, we prided ourselves on a national economy that was breaking new records with each passing day — more goods, more services, more wealth, more consumption, more labor, more leisure.

Only now are we beginning to realize that we have paid a very heavy price for what we call progress. We assumed that increased production was itself a desirable achievement. Now we see that much of what we produce is meaningless or even negative in value. Professor Robert Lekachman writes in *Commentary* that if a new pulp plant pollutes a clean stream, gross national product increases not just by the value of the paper produced by the mill, but also by the value of the purifying devices that must be installed downstream to make the water usable once again. It is perhaps worth asking how much of the increase in the services sector of our economy is accounted for by dry cleaning facilities which thrive on increased air pollution.

We have produced a glut. The Affluent Society has become an Effluent Society. Our lives have been dedicated so mindlessly to increasing quantity that they have been decreasing in quality, almost in direct proportion to the increase in our gross national product. As Hobart Rowen, a columnist on economic affairs, says:

> It is not just the question of how much of our vaunted GNP consists of worthless appendages, like tail fins or gaudy chrome decorations, but how much of our product is actually destructive to life and health. Slowly but surely we have come to realize that *more* is not necessarily *better*, and this has even given rise to a far-out new school of "zero growth" advocates who suggest that the only thing we can do to help the environment is to stop future growth.

The issue of quantity vs. quality in American life has been joined. In a sense this entire book has been concerned with this one central problem. When we asked in Chapter 6, "What Kind of Society Do We Want?", we were trying to suggest that each of us as citizens contributes in many ways to the quality — or lack of it — of American life. We do this partly through the political process and partly through our activities in non-government institutions and in our private lives. We will return again to this central question in the final chapter, when we consider the paradox of our times, spiritual poverty amid material affluence.

Much of what we mean when we talk about the quality of American life has to do with the ways in which we use and abuse different but interrelated parts of our environment. The environment is lakes and air, wildlife and trees, mountains and river valleys. But it is also sidewalks and skyscrapers, automobiles on superhighways, dams and public housing — and people. All these make up the world in which we live, and the quality of American life deteriorates when people are crowded into unhealthy slum tenements just as surely as when our air is fouled with industrial smoke and automobile exhaust. To mount a realistic campaign to restore the quality of our environment, we will ultimately have to deal with such disparate problems as urban noise, agricultural wastes, family planning, the technology of mass-produced, low-cost housing, the ecological balance of deserts and swamps, gun controls, inadvertent weather modification, traffic patterns, planned cities, alternative sources of energy, and criminal rehabilitation.

But if there is one catalyzing issue that has brought the question of quality into dramatic focus, it has been the growing abuse of our natural environment — our air, water, and land. The newspaper datelines of the Sixties — Birmingham, Selma, Watts, Detroit — were associated with civil rights and race riots; the list of the Seventies may begin with names like Santa Barbara, Lake Erie, the Everglades, and the Cuyahoga. Americans of all ages are coming to realize that our great and growing national wealth has brought with it not only growing inconvenience, overcrowding, and filth, but a potential threat to our very existence as a species. We now understand that we must restore its balance and clean it up, whatever the cost, if we are to continue to inhabit the face of the earth. If we do not, as Dr. David Gates warned in testimony before a House Subcommittee in the 90th Congress, "we will go down in history as an elegant technological society struck down by biological disintegration for lack of ecological understanding."

As a public issue, pollution has hit with such force and suddenness that at times the dimensions of the problem seem overwhelming. The sheer volume of information has polluted us with words. It will be easier to understand and deal with the problem if we try to break it down into its major components — air, water, and land.

A *New Yorker* cartoon not long ago pictured a wife sitting down to dinner out on the terrace of a high-rise apartment and calling impatiently to her husband, "Hurry, dear, your soup is getting dirty." Time was when air pollution could appropriately be treated with gentle humor. But on 16 January 1970, the *Chicago Tribune* carried a front-page banner headline saying "POLLUTION BLANKETS CITY." The story said the bad air came from industrial areas of South Chicago and Gary, and that it actually dimmed the sunlight though no clouds were overhead. In some areas of the city the sulphur dioxide gas count went as high as .24 parts per million for a 24-hour period; health problems begin to develop for infants, the elderly, and persons suffering from respiratory ailments at a count of only .11 parts per million over a 24-hour period. During the preceding November, the death rate of tracheal bronchitis in children had doubled in the seven-day period after sulphur dioxide pollution rose to similar levels. Perhaps we are not as far as we might have thought from the grim prophecy found in Revelation 9:

> . . . and from the shaft rose smoke like the smoke of a great furnace, and the sun and the air were darkened with the smoke from the shaft . . . By these three plagues a third of mankind was killed, by the fire and smoke and sulphur issuing from their mouths (RSV).

U.S. News and World Report estimates that America's automobiles, power plants, and factories annually release more than 140 million tons of toxic exhausts into the atmosphere. The problem is most serious in our large urban areas, choked with both cars and factories. Automobile-induced smog in Los Angeles is so severe that school children are often not permitted to exercise outside, and pine trees are dying on mountainsides a full sixty miles to the east. Conventional wisdom has it that to breathe for half a day in New York City is equivalent to smoking a pack of cigarettes. The Public Health Service warns that air pollution has become "a contributory cause of cancer and a serious irritant to lung and respiratory tissue."

It is estimated that two-thirds of the air pollution hanging over American cities is due to cars. The culprit is the internal combustion engine, which annually emits more than eighty million tons of nitrogen oxides, carbon monoxide, hydrocarbons, and other fumes into the air. People laughed when the first bills seeking to ban internal combustion engines were introduced in the California State Legislature not long ago. We cannot afford to laugh anymore. American science and technology are going to have to find a fumeless substitute. Engines fueled by natural gas have been tried in some federal government cars. Other possible engines might utilize steam, electricity, turbine propulsion, or a low-emission fuel.

Pesticides, herbicides, and other sprays are another source of serious air pollution. A contemporary protest poster warns that the milk of nursing mothers may contain DDT in the amount of .10 to .30 parts per million, or two to six times the amount considered safe for commercial sale. It shows the breast of a pregnant mother, with the words "Caution — keep out of reach of children." In Globe, Arizona, a leader of the Informed Citizens Union, complaining about the use of herbicide sprays to eliminate chaparral, told the UPI, "People who weren't sick before are sick now. Women are having hemorrhaging troubles, poultry and dogs have died, and livestock are born deformed or dead."

Former Secretary of Health, Education and Welfare Robert Finch put stringent controls on the use of DDT and other pesticides pending further investigations. But the job of cleaning up our nation's air will require vast resources in the years ahead. Senator Henry Jackson estimates that it may cost between twelve and fifteen billion dollars over the next five years. His figures may be conservative; *Time* puts the probable cost at sixty billion.

Water pollution is a second scourge on the American environment. The state of Ohio boasts three great waterways, the Ohio River, Lake Erie, and the Cuyahoga River. *Newsweek* rates the Ohio as America's filthiest river. For years Erie has been what environmentalists call a dead lake. And in the summer of 1969 the Cuyahoga River caught fire, burning two railroad trestles in the process. Inland waterways have not been the only casualties; commercial oil spills off the coast of Santa Barbara sent a slimy black death onto the beaches of Southern California, focusing national attention on the widespread destruction of wildlife and the fouling of the sea.

Interior Secretary Walter Hickel considers water pollution our number one environmental problem. Every year Americans dump several hundred million tons of industrial and domestic wastes into our lakes and streams. An additional 1.3 billion tons of manure and refuse from agricultural feed lots pollute our rural waters, and acid mine drainage contributes several hundred million tons. We have already driven fish and other wildlife from many of our lakes and streams, and we are in the process of inadvertently destroying the wetlands and estuarine marshes where they breed.

We need water for drinking, sanitation, recreation, and industrial use as well as the ecological balance of our wildlife population. These needs will increase dramatically in the next thirty years. But we are running out of sources of water pure enough for these purposes. A massive program to build industrial and municipal waste treatment facilities, separate storm and sanitary sewer systems, and desalination and recycling plants may ease the shortage, but according to most estimates this will require as much as thirty billion dollars over the next five years.

We are despoiling our land as well as befouling our air and water. Much of this problem stems from our colossal failure to deal with solid wastes. The average American produces more than five pounds of solid refuse per day, in human waste, glass bottles and tin cans, plastic bags and broken or worn out utensils and playthings. Nearly eighty percent of this waste is dumped, clogging our rivers and leaving eyesores on the outskirts of our towns. Most of the rest is burned, further polluting our filthy air. More sophisticated methods of sanitary landfill and emission-reduced incineration have proved effective in reducing the problem, but their use is not yet widespread. Composting gives evidence of being a valuable way to deal with organic waste, including paper, but municipal waste technology is still in its infant stage. We desperately need a means of completely recycling the end products of virtually all consumption if we are not to be buried beneath our own garbage.

We ravage our land in other ways. Fifteen million tons of scrapped automobiles litter our countryside. Unregulated, unesthetic advertising hides our forests and fields from the highways. Our roads themselves are often monuments to bad taste; as Ian McHarg, colorful conservationist at the University of Pennsylvania, says:

> There are other aspirants who vie to deface shrines and desecrate sacred cows, but surely it is the highway commissioner and the engineer who most passionately embrace insensitivity and Philistinism as a way of life and profession.

McHarg is even more incensed at the way in which we bulldoze our hillsides and fields, silting our rivers and losing more than one billion dollars annually in soil value due to erosion. Man, he says, is "a blind, witless, low-brow anthropocentric clod who inflicts lesions upon the earth."

There seems to be little question that the crux of the pollution problem is people. To paraphrase Commodore Oliver Hazard Perry, "We have met the enemy, and they are us." The destruction of our forests, pollution of our waters, scarring of our fields and hills, and fouling of our air have increased in proportion to the growth of our population. If we are going to make any real progress in the campaign to save our environment, we will have to take steps both to limit our own numbers and to change our attitudes about man in nature and in society.

In *The Population Bomb*, Dr. Paul Ehrlich paints a gloomy picture of an overcrowded, famine-prone world whose 3.5 billion population is now doubling at the incredible rate of once every thirty-seven years. Pollution problems, let alone food problems, increase geometrically when the population grows at such a rate. President Nixon recognized the urgency of bringing these numbers under control when he established the National Commission on Population Growth and the American Future in 1969. Our society can no longer afford the luxury of believing that only other nations need to worry about family planning. We have to be more thoughtful about bringing children into the world if we are to leave them a world worth inheriting.

136

While we take steps to limit our population growth, we must also begin to attack the specific problems of pollution in our air, water, and land. In his 1970 State of the Union Message, President Nixon said:

> The great question of the '70's is: Shall we surrender to our surroundings or shall we make our peace with nature and begin to make reparations for the damage we have done to our air, to our land, and to our water?

The President shortly thereafter offered a comprehensive multi-billion-dollar program for reclaiming our environment. New proposals for air and water pollution control, solid waste management, parklands and recreation were included in seven environmental bills which he sent to the Congress.

The program calls for a truly national effort, a two-pronged campaign by government and private industry. Funds for treatment facilities will come from both the public and private sectors, but it will be the particular responsibility of industry to innovate and of government to regulate. Thus private enterprises are being encouraged to develop alternatives to the internal combustion engine, and new means of treating industrial wastes and thermal pollution. If the bills pass, the federal government will have broad new powers to enforce anti-pollution standards and to punish violators with fines of up to $10,000.00 per day.

The private citizen must also play an important role along with government and industry if we are to mount an effective national campaign. Above all there must be a change in basic attitudes toward production and consumption. Much of the current outcry against pollution in America is tinged with a kind of environmental paranoia, a delusion of persecution, a feeling that somehow sinister forces are trying to destroy our earth and any chance we might have to enjoy it. Who causes pollution? According to the environmental paranoids it is always *them* — the corporate giants, the utility companies, the Army Corps of Engineers, the Atomic Energy Commission, and so on. Some of the names have undoubtedly made a substantial contribution to our pollution problems, but it is neither useful nor accurate to pretend that they are out to despoil our environment. They serve the public — us. As consumers we are just as guilty as those who provide us with goods and services. We must be willing to admit that we are all polluters, and that we have been destroying ourselves.

Perhaps more than anything else, we as a people need a new appreciation of our own relationship to the world of nature. Environmental scientists like to speak of "ecosystems" — delicately balanced relationships between two or more kinds of living things which need each other to survive. Dr. John Cantlon, a leading American ecologist, has said that man's psychological history has been shaped by three great discoveries. Copernicus, in showing that the earth moves around the sun, proved that man's world was not the physical center of the universe. Darwin, finding natural links between animal species, showed that man was perhaps not as separate from the world of nature as he had wanted to believe. Now in our times ecologists are discovering that far from dominating nature, man depends on a subtle natural balance of forces for his very survival. He cannot put himself outside nature and continue to live. As Dr. Rene Dubos says in *The Environmental Handbook:**

> The phrase "health of the environment" is not a literary invention. It has real biological meaning, because the surface of the earth is truly a living organism. Without the countless and immensely varied forms of life that the earth harbors, our planet would be just another fragment of the universe with a surface as drab as that of the moon and an atmosphere inhospitable to man.

Thus we are discovering that the last frontier is in fact the first — our earth itself, the world of nature. We now have to educate ourselves to appreciate that world and our own place in it. I believe Christians should be able to point the way to this rediscovery, for it is our conviction that the earth is the Lord's, and the fulness thereof, man, and all they that dwell therein. The ecosystems through which man relates to other parts of the natural world are the very handiwork of God.

Some scholars and writers have recently suggested that it is the Judaeo-Christian tradition which has led us to such wanton despoliation of the earth. Citing Genesis 1:26, where God gave to man "dominion over the fish of the sea, and over the birds of the air, and over the cattle, and over all the earth," they argue that Christians ever after have taken this as a mandate to exploit the natural world.

But such a view is in direct contradiction to the other great commission God gave man in the garden: "Be fruitful, and multiply, and replenish the earth." This clearly demands the careful stewardship and cultivation of resources, which after all are God's and not man's. If

*Ballantine Books, New York, 1961. Page 27.

anything, we have failed in that stewardship, and the time has come to rededicate ourselves to fulfilling the original commission. As Lutheran theologian Joseph Sittler has said, "Reason says that destroying clean air is impractical. Faith ought to say it is blasphemous."

As Christians, I believe we have an explicit responsibility to speak continually to the issue of quality in our national life, and more important, to make clear that the quality of our environment cannot be measured or described in physical terms alone. It will do little good to reclaim our air, our water, and our land, if as a nation we continue to abuse our hearts, our minds, and our souls. There could be no more direct warning on this point than the example cited by the prophet Zephaniah, who cried:

> Woe to her that is filthy and polluted, to the oppressing city!
> She obeyed not the voice; she received not correction; she trusted not in the Lord; she drew not near to her God (Zephaniah 3:1,2).

OUTREACH

The first three sections of this book have dealt with origins, institutions, and issues. In the final section I would like to take up the theme of outreach, to ask what the role of the Christian might be in solving some of the problems we have discussed, and hopefully to suggest some answers.

Chapter 17 is an examination of what I consider to be one of the most debilitating debates in Christendom — the argument between liberals and evangelicals about which is more important, personal salvation or social concern. To me it seems clear that either without the other is dead, and I have tried to suggest ways in which committed Christians can seek to combine the two in forging a new Christian social ethic. The next chapter discusses the broader mission of the church, abroad as well as at home. The final chapter is in some ways the most personal of any chapter in this book. It is the testament of a Congressman who feels that there is only one real answer to the paradox of our times, and that it can be found only in the Person of Christ.

17
TOWARD
A NEW
CHRISTIAN
SOCIAL
ETHIC

It is a demonstrable fact of American life that the liberal religious community tends to be liberal on economic and political questions, while the conservative religious community tends to be conservative in economics and politics. Some believe this merely shows that liberal and conservative viewpoints are essentially psychological, whereas others maintain that there are definite ideological links between these points of view. Do the basic doctrinal differences between the liberal and conservative religious communities imply that to maintain ideological consistency, the same basic differences must inevitably and inexorably be transferred to attitudes about society and politics? I think that this is an extremely relevant and important question that has had only limited attention.

To answer this question properly, we must put it in historical perspective. America's religious heritage was essentially individualistic and Protestant. The majority of our early settlers were the original WASPS (White-Anglo-Saxon-Protestants), who stressed that man's relations with the outer world could be made perfect only insofar as the inner man was in harmony with God. The way to change the social order was not through institutions, but by changing the individuals that made up the social order itself.

This doctrine was strongly reinforced by Christian orthodoxy, which emphasized that (1) man was a sinner, and in his own person he could achieve no perfection, and (2) the kingdom of God was a spiritual kingdom, and therefore distinct from and superior to the earthly and temporal kingdoms of man. Many scholars have pointed out that the Constitution itself reflected this thinking, in that it defined clear limits to the purpose of government and built in a system of checks and balances. Man was a sinner and could not be trusted with unlimited power. Here we have a clear religious basis for limited government.

At the end of the nineteenth and the beginning of the twentieth century, there were sweeping changes in American society which had a significant impact on the religious community. Industrialization and urbanization created social problems of such magnitude that individuals felt increasingly helpless in the midst of this mass-oriented new technological society. This fact, combined with the impact of rising scientific skepticism about religion in general, brought many religious leaders to the point where they repudiated the established doctrines of the church in an attempt to remake Christianity into a thoroughly modern expression suitable for twentieth-century man.

This movement within the religious community is sometimes referred to as liberalism or modernism, but it is most often described as the social gospel movement. Its major theme is that inner religious piety is not an adequate response to the crushing problems of technological and urban society. Personal piety cannot deal with mass unemployment or the effects of economic recession. Nor can it provide a theoretical framework from which to cast judgment on the great social issues of the day.

Had the social gospel movement stopped here, there would probably have been no major problem. But it went beyond a rejection of the old frontier individualism that characterized earlier American history and developed into a wholesale attack on Protestant orthodoxy. The social gospel movement fell captive to the prevailing nineteenth-century notion of the perfectibility of man (in contrast to the orthodox conception of man as sinner), and it emphasized the sacredness of our created earthly existence to the point of virtually repudiating any concept of a transcendent and eternal kingdom of God (thereby destroying the old Augustinian distinction between the City of God and the City of Man).

Thus, while there was much that was good in the social gospel movement, insofar as reawakening the social conscience of the Christian church was concerned, there was much that ran counter to basic Christian teachings themselves. In the attempt to be modern and relevant, the social gospel movement finally went on to deny the inspiration of the Bible, miracles such as the virgin birth of Christ, and the belief in Christ's second return to earth.

It could only be a matter of time until such thinking produced severe reactions from within the religious community itself. The fundamentalist movement began in response to the threat posed by the social gospel to orthodox Christian belief.

This threat pushed the orthodox community into almost a wholly defensive posture. I have some very vivid recollections from boyhood of sermons preached in what was then called the Swedish Free Church of Rockford, Illinois. "Modernism" was the great archenemy of the church of Jesus Christ, seeking to corrupt believers and divert their attention from the cross of Christ and man's need of salvation. It was continually cited as evidence of the apostasy of the age.

We can see in retrospect that many of the great problems which plague us today were already in evidence then, but our entire attention was diverted to battling those whom some fundamentalists believed were simply advance men for the anti-Christ because of the false doctrine which they espoused. We were reminded that even as Paul had to cleanse the church at Corinth of those who sought to promulgate error in their explanation of the Resurrection, and to warn the church at Colossae against Gnosticism, fundamentalists had to defend historic Christianity against the siege guns of "Modernism." We were at that time so concerned with the preservation of the distinctive doctrines of our faith, that we failed to devise ways in which to exercise these doctrines in the modern world. For example, in the "Fundamentals," a series of tracts that were widely distributed during the height of the fundamentalist controversy, not one of the roughly one hundred tracts dealt with a social issue, except for passing references to the Communist situation in the Soviet Union.

In the religious debate between these two factions, a sort of "guilt by association" began to set in. Those concerned about relating Christian belief to the social sector were ostracized from the fundamentalist community, on the assumption that they were religious radicals as well. Debate over social ethics became a subterfuge for a more serious debate over the meaning of Christianity itself.

But many of the shibboleths of religious modernism were shattered by the judgment of history. The Great Depression, two World Wars, a cold war, and widespread revolution made men wonder if peace could ever be instituted on earth. The failure of many liberal welfare and aid programs called into question man's ability to solve social and human problems by institutional change. Slowly the steam went out of the social gospel movement.

With the decline of the social gospel, the religious situation became more fluid. Many former liberals began to reaffirm much of the orthodox position, to the point where they started to call themselves neo-orthodox. In the conservative camp, the term *evangelical* began to replace the use of the word *fundamentalist*, for those who wanted to dissociate themselves from the excesses of some of the fundamentalist zealots of the preceding thirty years. But the heritage of bitter fighting between the two communities remained. What ensued was a truce, rather than a definitive peace treaty in the religious cold war. In the process, the religious left — although chastened — continued to identify itself with the economic and political left. And the religious right continued to identify itself with the economic and political right.

The cooling of religious tempers gives us the opportunity today to break through this uncritical alignment of religious and political conservatism and religious and political liberalism. I, for one, have tried to take advantage of the ceasefire between these two warring camps to rearticulate what I think a concerned evangelical could and should stand for in the social arena.

To begin with, while I am essentially a religious conservative, I do not believe that religious conservatism must be equated with or regarded as synonymous with conservative solutions to all our political problems. One can cling to orthodox Christianity without denying the right of the poor to be clothed and fed, or the right of minorities to their civil rights, or that there is a proper role for government to assume in fighting poverty and promoting human rights. In fact, I would reverse this statement to say that it is difficult for me to believe that a Christian can not be concerned and compassionate about these problems.

I would without hesitation maintain that man is a sinner, and that all of his social institutions are affected by sin. Ultimate social change depends upon changing man himself, and man himself cannot be changed simply by redesigning or altering his environment. If that were true, Christ's death on the cross would have been completely unnecessary, and the whole rationale of God's plan for man's redemption would collapse. Believing as I do that Christ's words to Nicodemus are relevant to the situation of modern man, and that we must be born again, in no way relieves me of my responsibility to pursue social justice, to act in compassion toward my fellow man, and to seek a better world. For, while man is a sinner, God has implanted within each of us a conscience, and with it we become responsible for our own actions and chargeable with the responsibility to do mercy, seek justice, and walk humbly before our God. We cannot escape the fact that we are our brother's keeper.

I believe that the perfect society will always pass us by. I will not accept the utopian theories of either the classless Communist society, or the perfect democratic way of life envisioned by our own American theorists at the turn of the century. Perfection in personal and social relations is something reserved for the kingdom of God. And therefore, as Christians, we owe our ultimate responsibility toward that higher and eternal order. But our religious belief must never become a proprietary drug that we ingest, so that we somehow become immune to the misery that flows all around us. This is the kind of religion which Lenin speaks of, scornfully, as the opiate of the masses. We are called to be the light of the world, the salt that gives life its savor.

I see no reason to deny the validity of the supernatural as the price that must be paid to take a sincere interest in the natural phenomena that operate in the sphere of our earthly existence. Indeed we are currently witnessing a tremendous upsurge of interest in the supernatural, the occult, and even obscure forms of Oriental mysticism by many who are simultaneously very active in political causes which relate wholly to the material side of man's existence. Although I believe that the ultimate course of history is governed by Divine Providence, as opposed to "human progress," I believe as well that God created us as human beings to participate fully in the drama of human history. This is part of the meaning of the Incarnation itself — God became man and acted out the drama of redemption within the framework of human affairs.

I also believe that we of the conservative religious community have for too long been merely reacting against the past excesses of the social gospel movement. We must begin to think critically about the relation of our faith to the opportunities and obligations of twentieth-century life. Faith in action needs to become our motto, and we need to become sensitized to our proper role in ministering to the needs of our fellowmen. "Bear ye one another's burdens, and so fulfil the law of Christ" (Galatians 6:2).

Conservative theology does place limits on the hope and faith we can place in human institutions. As Christians, we must not, I repeat, succumb to the illusion that all man needs to do is restructure his environment. We recognize that basic to ultimate social change is the necessity that man have a new nature, that he become a new creature in Christ. "For in Christ Jesus neither circumcision availeth any thing, nor uncircumcision, but a new creature" (Galatians 6:15). But this does not deny our obligation to bring social institutions to the limits of perfection possible within the framework of an unregenerate society. Rather, it demands it. I, for one, hope that we do not allow this opportunity to pass us by.

While I personally have high regard for the individualistic heritage of the evangelical, I believe its major weakness has been that it fails to see that sin and righteousness are social issues with social dimensions, as well as personal issues with personal dimensions. The Old Testament writers, for example, spoke often of the consequences of the sins of the fathers spilling over into the third generation. We must come to the point of realizing that personal ethics cannot be separated from social ethics; you cannot have one without the other.

Because Christians are not "of the world," they have too often tended to act as if they are not "in the world," and practiced a pietistic separation. Their separation from those things they believe to be evil has too often been an excuse for separation from those things that are good. Thus, while they have made abstinence from alcohol and tobacco signs of their commitment, they have often abandoned their responsibilities in the world of literature and the arts, and, as I have pointed out many times elsewhere in this volume, in the field of government itself.

Too often evangelicals have allowed the "don't do this" mentality to dominate their ethical thinking. This approach is no better than that of the new moralists who say "do anything you want, so long as you do it with the right intentions." In contrast to both these views of ethics, Christ's approach was positive and instructive. He told us what we should do, not just what we should not do.

Thus, I think the evangelical community can be fairly criticized for its failure to devise a genuinely positive and constructive social ethic. We have been reacting against the social gospel. As an excuse for a non-contributing role, we cling to an exceedingly individualistic heritage. We do suffer from withdrawal symptoms. We do still have an essentially negative approach to the very real problems of many of our neighbors.

The Reverend George Perry, former president of the theologically conservative National Negro Evangelical Association, made this point recently in talking about the Billy Graham Crusades: "We believe in the content of the Graham message, but we can't go along with its suburban, middle-class, white orientation that has nothing to say to the poor nor to the black people . . . . We preach the whole gospel to man, a perfect marriage of the social gospel and theological, Bible-believing Christianity."

However, we can be thankful that there is an evident change of opinion and approach making itself felt within the evangelical com-

munity. Some new directions are taking shape, as we rethink our obligations in and to society. To this new thrust I would like to add some
thoughts on the creation of a new and vital evangelical social ethic.

1. We need to develop a Christian social ethic that looks both to
the need of the human heart and the inner man, and to man's external
relations, to both the spiritual and the physical elements in life. We
should lead the way in creating an integrated ethical system that reunites
personal responsibility with social responsibility, and yet remains true
to the demands of the Gospel.

2. We need a more positive outlook toward government. As evangelicals, we have tended to have a negative attitude toward government.
This, it seems to me, is contrary to Scripture, which tells us that government is an institution ordered by God as an instrument of justice. Just
because we do not regard government as the panacea for all our social
ills, does not mean that we fail to recognize the fact that government is
one of the fundamental orders of creation, and therefore deserves our
respect as Christians every bit as much as marriage and the family.

3. We need a more realistic view of politics. There is in American
culture a sort of mythological caricature of the corrupt, calculating
politician. We must recognize that politics is no more corrupt or cor-
rupting than many other professions — that the corruption manifests
itself in a different manner. In fact, it is perfectly logical to argue that
politics may be less corrupt, because it is subject to public scrutiny.
There is a famous statue of the great humorist Will Rogers at the entrance
to Statuary Hall in the United States Capitol. He is facing down the
corridor in the direction of the House Chamber. Legend has it that he
wanted to be placed in that position so that he could keep an eye on the
Congress which he so often lampooned.

I was asked some time ago to pass judgment on the proposed plot
of a Christian movie dealing with young people who entered politics,
only to be confronted in a dramatic denouement at the end of the film
by the fact that the supposed hero-statesman was in fact a hypocritical
old-time, machine-style politician. This seems to me to be the wrong
way to orient Christian young people toward politics as a profession.

I wonder how many Christians reading these pages have ever held
political office, even as a precinct committeeman. If Christians leave
opportunities for participation open and unfilled, the void will be filled
by those who do not necessarily share a similar ethical concern. We

must be careful not to lose by default what could be won with some additional effort on our part.

Someone has said, "The church is filled with willing people — some of them willing to work and others willing to let them." Let none of us take refuge in the false notion that the problems of poverty and social injustice are the exclusive concern of the state.

To me it is a little sad that the radicalized intelligentsia of today has begun to embrace more and more of the organized church, its pastors, and leading laymen. Indeed, both the Catholic and the Protestant churches are now troubled by drop-outs from the ranks of the clergy. The church has become excessively programmatic in its approach to problems of social welfare and almost slavish in its belief that only government programs can remedy our problems.

One religious leader put it this way: "We Christianized the federal government because we wouldn't tithe to do the job ourselves." The average American today suffers no twinge of conscience when he passes the sick man on the road. He knows he has paid the Good Samaritan to come along after him and take care of this rather unpleasant social obligation. But the import of Christ's teaching is very plain. He expects us to take the role of the Good Samaritan, and not delegate our Christian love and compassion and concern in every instance to a paid professional or functionary. We are enjoined to love our neighbor — not just to pay taxes to employ someone else to love our neighbor.

As a boy I sat through many an altar call for those willing to dedicate their lives to Christ on the foreign mission field. I trust that many will continue to heed a similar call, for undoubtedly the needs of the developing countries of the world are still great. However, I would also like to see some altar calls for men and women who would publicly dedicate themselves to help meet the needs in their home community. I believe the church needs to get very specific about this and sharpen the challenge to all of us who call ourselves Christians to really find a place of service. It may not be full time; perhaps part time in a school, hospital, or out-patient clinic. The needs are legion, They could be inventoried very quickly through the help of a local Community Welfare Council or a Red Feather agency.

The Scriptures teach tithing of our incomes. What a wonderful blessing would be wrought if we also believed in time tithing; if we believed and practiced the idea that it was equally important to share our time. The churches of our nation annually engage in "One Great

Hour of Sharing" when funds are collected for the poor, the hungry, and the deprived. How noble an experiment it would be if our churches would also promote a program of "One Great Hour of Sharing" in which we would actually give our time, that most precious of all commodities, on a regular weekly or semi-weekly basis to help solve some of the staggering problems that threaten our society.

Some will immediately say, "But where would we go, and what would we do?" Others will undoubtedly scoff about the do-gooders who merely end up getting in each other's way. The inertial force that would have to be overcome to launch such a project on a national scale cannot be underestimated, but I would like to see the evangelical church in our land in the forefront of just such an effort. I would like to see the Christian leaders of our time devoting their creative talents to attempting to mobilize resources within the 320,000 churches that make up the organized religious community of our nation.

It may well be said at this point that all this is unnecessary and merely adds another layer to the religious bureaucracy that already exists. We now have local, state, and national church organizations and councils of one kind or another, and indeed even a World Council of Churches. However, these groups have in my opinion signally failed to secure the active participation on a time-sharing basis of the millions of communicants whom they nominally represent. The job is not getting done. Indeed recent hard evidence suggests a significant waning of their financial support as proof of a lack of enthusiasm for what they have accomplished. At a time when many clergymen are talking more than ever before about the necessity of immersing ourselves in social and political problems, the responses grow ever weaker.

I believe a large part of the problem is the inability of the average member of an affluent suburban church to really feel much empathy for the problems of an inner city world so remote from his own existence. In an interview in the April, 1970, issue of "Psychology Today," the liberal theologian and Harvard Divinity School professor, Harvey Cox, alleges that we have "inherited a perverted form of Christianity, deodorized and afraid of smell." I am afraid that there are a great many modern Christians who, if our Lord suddenly returned and they found Him dining with the publicans and sinners who infest the big city slums, would recoil with the same fastidious horror as did the Pharisees and Sadducees two thousand years ago. Yet Henry Drummond, in his great sermon "The City Without a Church," reminds us that:

City life is human life at its intensest, man in his most real relations. And the nearer one draws to reality, the nearer one draws to the working sphere of religion. Wherever real life is, there Christ goes. And He goes there, not only because the great need lies there, but because there is found, so to speak, the raw material with which Christianity works . . . the life of man. To do something with this, to infuse something into this, to save and inspire and sanctify this, the actual working life of the world, is what He came for. Without human life to act upon, without relations of men with one another, of master with servant, husband with wife, buyer with seller, creditor with debtor, there is no such thing as Christianity. With actual things, with Humanity in its everyday dress, with the traffic of the streets, with gates and houses, with work and wages, with sin and poverty, with these things, and all the things and all the relations and all the people of the City, Christianity has to do, and has more to do than with anything else.

Several years ago a Presidential task force reported on national voluntary services. It began its report with the conclusion that "millions of Americans are willing to serve their less fortunate countrymen, but have no national rallying force to challenge them." It went on to say that it was the Office of the President of the United States alone that could summon them to action. Somehow, I cannot agree that this office, important as it is and entitled to the great dignity and honor that it is, is the only vehicle.

The Church of Jesus Christ ought to play a part in rallying Christians to social action. Indeed, as we noted in an earlier chapter on "What Kind of Society Do We Want," it is only as we play this kind of role that we will get the type of society that, as Christians, we would like to see. The church can and should encourage social and economic change. We are living in an age when, to paraphrase the late President Kennedy, every Christian should in effect be an officeholder.

I once heard President Nixon state the goals of his administration in terms of three R's. He listed them as Reorganization, Renewal, and Restoration. I'm still old-fashioned enough in my theology to believe that the three R's of the church are Redemption, Regeneration, and Renewal. We must begin to construct a new, vital Christian social ethic and tradition, which can give us the moral foundation on which to build an America capable of achieving its national goals.

18
THE MISSION OF THE CHURCH IN A TROUBLED WORLD

We have written at some length of the great, perhaps unprecedented problems facing our society as we enter the Seventies, and of the particular responsibility that Christians have to develop a revitalized social ethic which will encourage Christian contributions to the solution of those problems. What of our responsibility in the world beyond our own society? Has the mission of the church — "Go ye and preach the gospel to every creature" — changed amid the turbulent wars and rumors of war that have cast their long shadows over the earth in this bloodiest century in the history of man?

The story is told of a German church that was destroyed during World War II. Later when the rubble was being cleared away, a statue of Christ was found with only the hands missing. A famous sculptor offered to restore the hands, but the officers of the church declined, saying that this was a symbol of our Lord's dependence on the hands of His followers to serve Him in loving concern and compassion for others. In today's troubled world, that commission and that mandate are more vitally needed than they have ever been before.

Christ commissioned those who took Him at His word to be the salt of the earth, and I interpret that to mean exactly what it says. We are asked to witness to His love, His grace, His redeeming power in whatever place and in whatever circumstances we find ourselves. For many of us that means in relatively small American communities where most people have already heard the good news of the Gospel. For others, it means in great foreign cities where the traditions, pace of life, and preoccupations of the people all militate against their receiving the Gospel of Christ. Our world is smaller and more aware of its own faraway corners than the world of our parents' day. Thus, none of us, even if we have never been abroad, can escape the responsibility of being "the salt of the earth."

To the extent that this is true, we have to modify our traditional image of that great hero of the church, the foreign missionary. It is not at all that his role is now redundant or empty (we will say more about that role in a moment). Rather, as the world has become smaller, each of us has become more involved with people in other parts of it. We become, in a totally unprogrammed way, missionaries in the sense that literally the whole world is now watching us day by day, measuring our actions against what we say we believe. We are witnesses, whether we think of it that way or not, to the God we profess and to the kind of lives we are pledged to lead because we believe in Him.

If we are honest, this should make us think twice about the way we have viewed foreign missions in the past. I fear that all too often we have seen them as a means of salving our consciences for not responding to the needs of those close to us. As Screwtape says to his young apprentice in *The Screwtape Letters**:

> Do what you will, there is going to be some benevolence, as well as some malice, in your patient's soul. The great thing is to direct the malice to his immediate neighbors whom he meets every day, and to thrust his benevolence out to the remote circumference, to people he does not know. The malice thus becomes wholly real, and the benevolence largely imaginary.

In trying to reach an informed understanding of the church's mission in today's world, we need not only an honest picture of our own motives, but a realistic view of the world, not just as it seems to us, but as it must look to those in other nations to whom we would make the Gospel meaningful. We live in a world where new barriers rise to separate men faster than old ones are broken down. One of the most familiar barriers is the longstanding tension between Communist-bloc nations and the democracies of the West. It has so dominated our feelings about other countries that we rarely try to understand either the underlying differences in philosophy, or the similarities and the possibilities for human contact, between people on both sides of what Winston Churchill called the Iron Curtain.

---

*C. S. Lewis, *The Screwtape Letters and Screwtape Proposes A Toast* (Macmillan, New York, 1961), Page 37.

And yet recent events have shown that this one great East-West conflict, which has ordered our view of the world and often provided a legitimate sense of national purpose in international relations, is no longer sufficient to explain the divisions that separate nations and lead men to unreasoning hatred of each other and each other's sons. In the remaining years of this century, I fear we may well see the growth of another source of tension and hatred among men. For want of a better phrase, I will call it the North-South conflict, though it is composed of many different factors.

The peoples of Asia, Africa, and Latin America are increasingly aware of the growing gulf between the rich nations and the poor nations, the developed and the underdeveloped. It happens that most of the poor nations of the world lie below the equator, in the southern hemisphere. Most of the world's rich and powerful nations lie north of the equator — the United States, Western Europe, the Soviet Union, Japan. The underdeveloped "southern" countries are coming to be known collectively as the "third world," because they stand outside the two great power blocs of the Communist East and the Democratic West.

There are three important features which unite these "third world" countries of the southern hemisphere and set them in potential conflict with the developed nations of the north. Most of the southern countries are primary-producing, or what we would call agricultural nations. Most of them are inhabited by colored peoples rather than white. Most of them are poor and many are getting poorer, relative to the powerful, industrialized nations of the northern hemisphere.

As the distinguished Swedish economist Gunnar Myrdal points out in his study of poverty among nations, *Asian Drama*, the roots of the growing disparity between rich and poor countries lie as much in the dynamics of slow cultural change and tradition-bound social organization, as in the requirements of technology and modern business enterprise. The world's most distinguished scholars have argued for years over what must be done to bridge this yawning gap between rich and poor nations. But the ordinary people of Asia, Africa, and Latin America may be forgiven if they grow impatient with learned discourses on the dynamics of poverty. What they see is that the industrialized white nations of the north, many of them former colonial powers, are daily growing wealthier and more powerful, while they themselves struggle to maintain a minimum standard of living. Is it any wonder that, fueled by a communications revolution that daily gives people around the

155

world a clearer picture of how the other half lives, this situation breeds growing resentment against countries in the northern hemisphere.

In addition to this North-South conflict between rich and poor nations, there has been a literal explosion of regional and civil wars — in the Middle East, in Central America, in Southeast Asia, and in Africa. The day hardly passes that some new conflict does not find its way onto our television screens or the front pages of our newspapers. I sense that our world is more divided and more in conflict than it has been in many years. East against West, North against South, communism against democracy, rich against poor, Arab against Jew, nationalist against colonialist, Hindu against Moslem, black against white — how many different ways can the sons of God's earth be torn?

As Christians, we recognize that underlying all these tensions and hatreds among nations and tribes, and to some degree, responsible for them all, is the fact of sin in individual lives and the need for the redeeming love of Christ. International conflict is but the macrocosm of the petty jealousies, greeds, and hatreds of each one of us, and wars between states will be with us so long as avarice and ill-will eat at the hearts of individual men.

Is there a role for the church in a world like this? I believe there is. Yet as the world itself is in conflict, so there is controversy over the place of Christians overseas. "Go ye into all the world" is still the unmistakable commission of Christ, but, partly because of some of the trends we have described, the missionary's role today is significantly different than it was at the beginning of the great missionary effort that has taken the Gospel into almost every known corner of the world.

When David Livingstone entered the Congo basin with a small group of native African bearers who were more frightened than he was; when Adoniram Judson left England for an evangelist's mission to Burma; when Hudson Taylor first knocked on the gates of an alien and hostile Chinese city, the missionary's role was clear and precise. Despite the opposition of heathen kings and the ravages of disease and discomfort, the missionary's only concern was to preach the Gospel of Christ to whomever would listen. His methods were simple and direct; he had little help from others; he was easily recognized and his role was often resented but seldom misinterpreted.

Even in *Through Gates of Splendor*, Betty Elliot's magnificent portrait of her late husband Jim and his four martyred colleagues — even in this modern account of the inspiring mission to the Auca Indians, the role of the missionary is a familiar one. Despite the use of airplanes, the sophisticated techniques of Bible translation, the hours of training and preparation to do a job that had never been done before, the mission was essentially the same: to reach individual men and confront them with the Word of God and the Person of Christ.

Increasingly during the last decade, the traditional role of the missionary has come into question. Modern communications methods have revolutionized the spreading of the Word of God, and modern political and cultural tensions have made it more and more difficult for missionaries to work in many countries of the third world. The missionary's role is often misrepresented as "cultural imperialism." He is often seen, whether mistakenly or not, as the agent of American or Western interests, a threat to the cultural and social integrity of the people among whom he seeks to work. His leadership role in national churches is increasingly resented, questioned, and played down. His mission is still the same — to get the Word of God to those who have not heard; however, his methods and approach have changed in ways that might not be easily understood by David Livingstone or even Jim Elliot.

More than ever, the missionary is called upon to understand the people he has been chosen to serve; to listen as well as preach; to be dialectic rather than didactic. For practical reasons, as well as reasons of principle, he must be more aware than ever of the difference between artifacts of culture and testaments of faith — and he must be careful not to destroy or deprecate the former as he tries to encourage the latter. He must be aware of political currents and technological trends. He must be prepared to be resented for reasons that have nothing to do with the Gospel of Christ, as well as for those that do.

If anything, the role of the missionary in today's world is more crucial than ever before. If he acts in conscience, grace, and conviction, the modern missionary's impact on the hearts of men can do much to dampen the flames of hatred, racial mistrust, and resentment that have poisoned the wellsprings of hope in so many nations of the world.

19
THE
PARADOX
OF OUR
TIMES

When I contemplate the psalmist's prayer, "Peace be within thy walls, and prosperity within thy palaces" (Psalm 122:7), I am struck by the paradoxes in American life today.

There is more prosperity in more homes than ever before in the history of our nation: more color television sets, more stereos, more cars, more electrical appliances, and so on. We are proud of our tremendous productive capacity as a nation. The Gross National Product in 1969 was a staggering $932.7 billion. The average per capita personal income after taxes in 1968 was $2928, compared to $1937 only eight years ago.

Along with this almost unbelievable prosperity, we have the most sophisticated technology in the world. We have achieved the age-old dream of putting a man on the moon. We are experimenting with ways of maintaining human life under the sea. We can predict when a storm will hit a certain locality. We have progressed from rather crude mechanical cotton pickers to lettuce pickers that are so sensitive they can tell whether or not a head of lettuce is firm enough to pick. There is hardly a minute of our lives that is not touched by the products of modern technology.

The psalmist talked about prosperity, and that is certainly relevant to us today. But the psalmist also talked about peace, something equally relevant, but something that consistently seems to elude our grasp.

Someone once said, "If wealth could buy happiness, Americans would be the happiest people in the world." But surely American life today shows dramatically that there is no causal relationship between prosperity and happiness. On the one hand, we have the easiest life ever in terms of material comforts and leisure time. On the other, there are more people seeking psychiatric help than ever before. Alcoholism is a real problem for a growing segment of the population. Millions of our high school and college students have used narcotics; recently the front page of the New York *Times* carried the picture of a twelve-year-old boy from the Bronx who had testified before a Committee of the New York Legislature that he was a heroin addict. Broken homes, desertions, and a general decline in sexual mores serve as more dramatic reminders of the failure of people to achieve peace and joy in their hearts. Like some terrible Old Testament plague, crime is increasing several times as fast as our population.

There seem to me to be two reasons for the paradox of our times. The first is the vanity of the mind, which rejects the need for spiritual change. Sometimes I think Communist thinkers understand the importance of a firm spiritual or ideological base far better than we do, even though their religion is one of secularism. During a visit here in Washington some years ago with Madame Chiang Kai-Shek, I asked her to explain the fanaticism of the rampaging Red Guards of Communist China. She said it was because Mao Tse-tung was intent on preserving the spirit of the revolution and of the famous "Long March" of 1934-36. He understood the importance of preserving the spiritual content of the revolution.

Historians say that during the most discouraging time of our own War for Independence, less than 500 people were willing to pledge their lives, fortunes, and sacred honor to the cause of the American Revolution, yet the spirit of those men who believed in the cause of freedom triumphed. There were only 120 Christians in the Upper Room in Jerusalem when the Holy Spirit came upon them, yet their fervor overcame all the vaunted power of Rome when the Empire attempted to destroy this nascent force that challenged the claims of paganism.

The whole history of the church down through the ages can be summed up in the words: "Faith is the victory!" It lives in spite of fire, dungeon, and sword. The Christian faith is viable not because it is something that we can postulate on the basis of conclusions derived from our scientific knowledge of man and the universe, but because it is the substance of things hoped for.

Why is it so hard for man to concede this vanity of the mind with which he is afflicted? After all, there are so many things that we do believe even though we do not understand. I once heard a lecture by Dr. Glenn Seaborg of the Atomic Energy Commission on man's first flight to Andromeda, our nearest star constellation, some two million light years away. At the speed of light, it would take men several years to get there. On returning from their voyage, because of the phenomenon of relativity, they would find that the earth had aged four million years

159

while they were away. Fantastic but believable. How much easier it ought to be to believe that there is a spiritual force that can change and transform the lives of men.

The second reason for the paradox of our times is the blindness of the heart, our lack of charity, our seeming inability to see the great needs that go unanswered. How else can we explain the fact that each night two-thirds of the world goes hungry, while in a country like America we cut the crust off our bread to make fancy sandwiches? How else can we explain the other incongruities of our affluent society? And yet this blindness of the heart is also related to the limitations of our finite minds. It is why we do not possess the infinite resources of compassion of our Lord, who cared equally for all men, who broke bread for men to eat, who healed men of their afflictions.

In his *Letters to Young Churches*, Phillips translates Romans 8:20 this way: "The world of creation cannot as yet see reality, not because it chooses to be blind, but because in God's purpose it has been so limited — yet it has been given hope." We don't choose to be blind, to be indifferent to the needs of an anguished world, yet we are limited in our vision and in the power of our minds. But the Apostle Paul does not simply leave us there. He does not just drop us to plunge endlessly and aimlessly in the vacuum of space. No, he says there is hope "that in the end the whole of created life will be rescued from the tyranny of change and decay" (verse 21).

General Carlos Romulo of the Phillipines, when President of the General Assembly of the United Nations, put it somewhat differently when he said, "We have harnessed the atom, but we will never make war obsolete until we find a force that can bridle the passions of men and nations." The only force that can accomplish this is not the power of the human mind; it will be the spiritual power of our Lord Jesus Christ translated into human actions that have become submissive to His will. We have deluded ourselves that we are on the threshhold of that great stage in man's development when he will free himself from the enslaving forces of his environment. Man cannot free himself from his own sinful nature.

The prophet Isaiah said, "Therefore my people go into exile for want of knowledge." We spend $34 billion on our elementary and secondary schools and other billions for higher education. The total federal contribution to education today approaches $12 billion. How can we say we have no knowledge? Haven't we been able to send a man to the moon? Later on in that same chapter, Isaiah declares, "Woe to those who call evil good and good evil, who put darkness for light and light for darkness, who put bitter for sweet and sweet for bitter!" To me, the prophet is warning against the kind of deliberate distortion of truth and the perversion of basic values that is really *no* knowledge. It represents the tragic ignorance of God's will for our lives and His wish that we live according to His plan for our lives.

We need dedicated Christians to communicate the fact that God's grace in Christ is the only force that can reconcile the hearts of men toward each other. To show forth God's love and grace, Christians have to be willing to stretch forth a helping hand, for example, to a black brother, not in condescension, but in Christian love. We need to become truly involved in community and political affairs to demonstrate that concern for all men which typified the ministry of our Lord.

Communications media experts like Marshal McLuhan insist that violence is endemic to our times, because man has lost his identity and is groping to find a new image in this new electronic culture. What those experts do not say, but what the Christian knows — and this ought to be his answer to a world that is desperately seeking solutions — is that it is only as we lose our identity and take on the *new nature* that is truly divine, will we be able to escape the corruption of the world and succeed in finding ourselves.

The Apostle Peter in 2 Peter 1:5-7 summarizes the fruit of that new nature imparted to us by Christ when we trust in Him: virtue, knowledge, temperance, patience, godliness, brotherly kindness, and charity. Let us, in Peter's words, be diligent in our calling, diligent in communicating by our deeds that we intend to be faithful to the task that our Savior has entrusted to us.

There are elements of the church desperately trying to relate to present needs. Much as we might disagree with their methods, we need to ask ourselves how well we are doing in communicating Christ's love to the present generation. We too must face the challenges of this generation with positive programs of outreach and help.

The late radio comedian Fred Allen once said, "Most Christians are people who spend six days sowing wild oats. On the seventh they go to church and pray for a crop failure." We need to make sure that those six days of the week when we are not in church are days when we are truly "showing forth" the ideals of our faith. It was Sam Shoemaker who observed that "Real Christian commitment doesn't take a man out of the world; rather, it drives him deeper into the world to seek to mend and heal it for Jesus' sake."

In dealing with the problems of poverty, race relations, and educational opportunity, we can use every kind of government program devised by the mind of man and still *fail*, unless we as individuals are willing to acknowledge our dependence upon God and live up to the two great commandments: "Thou shalt love the Lord thy God with all thy heart, and with all thy soul, and with all thy mind . . . . Thou shalt love thy neighbour as thyself" (Matthew 22:37,39).

William James, the American philosopher, said religion is either a dull habit or an acute fever. Many of us today hunger for commitment to a cause. We are bothered not just by social and environmental problems, but by an acute crisis of the spirit. To solve that, we need not just the work of a few professionals — ministers and youth workers — but of every Christian. Dr. Richard Halverson, in his book *Man to Man*,* makes this important point, "The Great Commission was not committed to a relatively few 'professionals,' but to the whole church. The work of the ministry belongs to the man in the pew, and it will never be done any other way."

Today there is moral poverty; there is spiritual want in our land, along with economic poverty. Many of our most talented young people are totally alienated. When I visited the Haight-Ashbury district of San Francisco, once the haven of countless hundreds of hippies, I saw there sad, vacuous, vacant, slack-jawed faces. Many of them were from affluent homes. They weren't suffering from material poverty, but from the spiritual poverty of their homes. Like the Bible's prodigal son, they were feeding on husks of drugs and living in a psychedelic haze.

Such is the paradox of our times, as we suffer the affliction of affluence. We are troubled in spirit, for ours is essentially a spiritual rather than a material crisis. We as yet only dimly perceive where the currents unleashed in our society are taking us.

A group of intellectuals met recently in New York to discuss "The Impotence of Power." Such an outpouring of pessimism you have never heard. There was an unrelieved litany of impending disaster and dark fears by those who spoke. Hannah Arendt gloomily decried the fact that our nation had fallen under a spell and nothing seemed to work any more. Only small governments can still rely on the support of their

*Published by Zondervan.

citizens and can still solve their problems, because only their problems are still manageable, she said. In a country as vast as the United States, the problems have simply become too immense.

Hans Morgenthau alleged that the majority was impotent; the government was impotent. "Majority rule," he said, "for which men have striven for centuries, has produced a situation in which men are more impotent, more powerless to influence their government than fifteen years ago."

I disagree with this mournful diagnosis; I take respectful exception. I believe there are changing attitudes toward a more positive outlook, both in government and out. To be sure we need to recognize the deep need for reforms in many of our present institutions of government. The Congress itself must become more responsive to the needs and challenges of our day.

Finally, the real solution to the paradox of our times will come if we as Christians help lead the way to a reaffirmation of basic spiritual values. We have a history and tradition as a Christian nation, but like Israel and Judah of old, we often tend to forget our dependence upon God and to substitute the ephemeral for the eternal.

In *Seven Storey Mountain*,* Thomas Merton concluded, "The world itself is no problem, but we are a problem to ourselves because we are alienated from ourselves." If I understand his point, it is that at the core of all our problems is the need for reconciliation. The Apostle Paul declared, "Through Him (Christ) God chose to reconcile the whole universe to himself, making peace through the shedding of his blood upon the cross — to reconcile all things, whether on earth or in heaven, through him alone" (Colossians 1:20, NEB).

This is our message to a needy world: the message that Christ died to bring reconciliation, to bring peace between men and God, and between men and their fellow-men. I believe this word of reconciliation is the answer to that search for some fundamental reassurance that is running so deeply throughout our land. This is the answer to the spiritual crisis that threatens to engulf us. It is the answer to what Archibald MacLeish calls "the bleakness and chaos of our time." Nowhere is it expressed more beautifully than in the words of our Lord, in John 16:33:

> I have told you all this so that in me you may find peace. In the world you will have trouble. But courage! The victory is mine; I have conquered the world (NEB).

*Harcourt, Brace & World, Inc., 1948.